NATURE at its STRANGEST

ARMY WORMS
(See page 60)

NATURE at its STRANGEST

TRUE STORIES from
the files of the Smithsonian
Institution's Center for
Short-Lived Phenomena

By **JAMES C. CORNELL, Jr.**

STERLING PUBLISHING CO., INC. NEW YORK

Oak Tree Press Co., Ltd. London & Sydney

OTHER BOOKS OF INTEREST

Strangely Enough
Weirdest People in the World
Would You Believe . .?: Useless Information
You Can't Afford to Be Without

All drawings by the author

© 1974, 1972 by James C. Cornell
Published by Sterling Publishing Co., Inc.
419 Park Avenue South, New York, N.Y. 10016
British edition published by Oak Tree Press Co., Ltd., Nassau, Bahamas
Distributed in Australia and New Zealand by Oak Tree Press Co., Ltd.,
P.O. Box J34, Brickfield Hill, Sydney 2000, N.S.W.
Distributed in the United Kingdom and elsewhere in the British Commonwealth
by Ward Lock Ltd., 116 Baker Street, London W 1
Manufactured in the United States of America
Library of Congress Catalog Card No.: 74–82336
Sterling ISBN 0–8069–3924–9 Trade   Oak Tree 7061–2038-8
3925-7 Library

CONTENTS

HOTLINE FOR SCIENCE

In this tiny, closed system that man calls home, every natural event, no matter how far away or how insignificant, becomes directly connected to our lives. For example, a volcano erupting in Bali may contribute air pollution to the skies over Chicago. An oil spill in Florida may destroy fish that feed the people of Canada.

Even the discovery of a lost tribe of Stone Age men is important to us, for their lives tell us how we evolved into a civilized society.

Gathering information about such far-flung and far-out events is the job of the Smithsonian Center for Short-Lived Phenomena. Since 1968 the Center has served as a unique news service providing fast, accurate information about earthquakes, volcanoes, fireballs, animal migrations, oil spills, sea surges, insect infestations, landslides, bird kills, lost tribe discoveries, and a host of other unusual, unpredictable, and often odd-ball events.

More than 2,000 scientists in 50 countries serve as correspondents in the Center's international network reporting news of far-out events in their far-flung corners of the world.

The stories in this book are not fiction. They are real-life events drawn from the files of the Smithsonian Center's headquarters in Cambridge, Massachusetts.

The events retold here occurred without warning and usually caught everyone, except the Center for Short-Lived Phenomena, completely by surprise. They were certainly sudden and unexpected, but you'd better believe them.

—James C. Cornell

THE SLEEPING GIANT AWAKES

An odd sound had awakened her in the middle of the long January night, and the housewife in the little seacoast village of Vestmannaeyjar on the island of Heimaey, Iceland, went downstairs for a predawn glass of warm milk. Just as she was about to return to bed, she saw a sight that would change her life forever.

The entire back yard of her home seemed on fire as red-hot liquid squirted out of the ground and flaming sky rockets shot up and over her house.

It was January 23, 1973, and the volcano Helgafell—dormant and silent for 7,000 years—had suddenly, violently, and incredibly awakened from its long sleep.

Since it forms the only above-water section of the Mid-Atlantic Ridge, Iceland is prone to all the stresses and strains usually found along the lines separating the earth's great crustal plates. Indeed, in this land of fire and ice, aircraft flights over the volcanoes are popular tourist attractions.

The Helgafell eruption proved no tourist attraction, however. More like a nightmare, it sent fountains of burning lava spurting 300 feet in the air. Huge black cinders, some as big as baseballs, rained down on the island. A vile, eye-burning, throat-searing cloud of smoke and gas rose three miles high. A steady river of lava flowed down the mountain into the port waters. And the constant scream of escaping steam, punctuated every few seconds by deafening explosions, caused intense, ear-splitting pain.

The lava heated the waters of the port and threatened to block its mouth, but the real threat to Heimaey residents was suffocation under the tons of ash and cinders that fell in a steady black blizzard. Luckily the local fishing fleet was in port on the day of the disaster; and, within twenty-four hours, almost everyone had been ferried to the mainland.

Observers arriving later saw a truly weird sight. With its street lamps still burning defiantly against the Arctic night, the deserted town of Vestmannaeyjar—once as bright and white and modern as any American suburb—lay under a thick blanket of black. Only the tips of street signs poked out above the 10-foot drifts of cinders. Some houses had collapsed under the weight; still others had burst into flames as the heat ignited oil storage tanks. And, looming over all, the fiery fountains of Helgafell continued to shoot skyward.

The eruption continued for several months, covering a three-square-mile area with lava and producing a central cone of lava more than 600 feet high. This cone, representing the new volcano spawned by the sleeping giant, was christened Kirkjufell, or "Church Hill."

The Kirkjufell eruption may be one of the best documented in history, with many observations made by some orbiting satellites. Only the 1963 eruption of the nearby volcano Surtsey ever received such intensive scientific attention.

Ironically, in 1963, when the hordes of scientists and reporters came to Iceland to watch the birth of Surtsey, their jumping-off point was the little village of Vestmannaeyjar and their transportation was the local fishing fleet. Now, many of these same observers had returned to witness the death of that village.

But, Vestmannaeyjar would not die that easily. When, in July, the eruption finally stopped, the people of Heimaey Island returned to survey the damage and assess the chances for rebuilding their lives. Those chances looked slim: Tons of ash covered much of the island, molten lava still carpeted the ground, and smoke and steam continued to drift upwards from cracks in the earth.

But the Icelanders are hardy people, long accustomed to the hardships of the Arctic weather and the unpredictable nature of their violent land. They dug out their homes and salvaged whatever remained of their possessions. Then, with typical ingenuity and economy, the Icelanders turned the volcano's fury to their advantage.

They used the very cinders that had buried their buildings to pave new roads and airport runways. Then, they tapped the molten lava of the volcano itself to provide a cheap source of heat and power. By January, 1974, one year after the first explosive yawns of that sleeping giant, new homes on Heimaey had been connected to water pipes heated by lava.

DIAMONDS FROM THE SKY

Maybe Finnish farmer Tor-Erik Andersson had heard about "pennies from heaven," but he certainly never imagined that diamonds could fall from the skies.

Andersson was tending crops on his farm near Haverö, Finland, one August day in 1971, when a loud and sudden noise rather like the combination of a jet plane and a thunderclap shattered the summer calm.

He could not think what had caused such a mysterious noise,

especially on a fine clear day. But his nine-year-old son came running from another part of the farmyard screaming that something had just crashed into the roof of the storehouse.

The entire Andersson family ran to the small building. Throwing open the door, they found the one-room shack filled with dust that swirled upwards in a thin shaft of bright sunlight. The sunlight came through a small ragged hole in the tile roof overhead. On the floor, spotlighted by the sunbeam and almost directly beneath the hole in the roof, sat a small wooden box with a small hole in its cover.

Cautiously, they opened the box. Inside lay a dark grey rock about the size of a plum. The thin outer crust of the rock had cracked to reveal a concrete-like interior.

Gingerly, farmer Andersson picked up the rock. It was unusually heavy for its size—about three pounds—and Andersson guessed, correctly, that it must be a meteorite. This chunk of cosmic debris, perhaps the remains of a former asteroid, had travelled countless millions of miles in deep outer space before entering the atmosphere over Haverö and finally falling through the roof of the storehouse and landing squarely inside this box.

However, an even more fantastic revelation was in store for the Anderssons—and scientists everywhere: Analysis of the rock showed that it contained traces of diamonds!

Diamonds found on earth are special carbon structures created by extremely high pressures deep within the ground. Diamonds found in meteorites, however, appear to result from the transformation of graphite (the lead used in "lead" pencils) by sudden shocks: perhaps the collision between the meteorite and other bodies in space. They are also extremely rare. Only six examples have been recorded since 1888.

Unfortunately, the Haverö meteorite didn't make the Andersson family very rich, despite its valuable contents. The weight of diamonds found in the meteorite was so small—it was in fact, almost microscopic—as to make it essentially worthless. Tor-Erik Andersson would be the first to agree that it is more profitable to raise grain than to try harvesting diamonds from the sky.

FOOLING THE FISHES

On the morning of January 28, 1971, thousands of the fish known as "mossbunkers" mysteriously died in Oyster Creek, New Jersey, about 60 miles south of New York City.

Because a large nuclear power plant operates on Oyster Creek, investigators from the Environmental Protection Agency hurried to the scene to see if the fish kill was somehow connected with the leakage of deadly radioactive wastes from the plant. The findings of the investigation were startling. The power plant *did* cause the deaths of the fish. But not by radiation poisoning. Or explosions. Or leakage of waste materials into the water. The poor unsuspecting fish were the victims of *thermal shock*, an unusual and unexpected danger of atomic plants that may be impossible to prevent.

Their first clue to the mystery of the dead fish came when investigators learned that because of mechanical problems the plant had shut down operations on January 27. Normally, one would think shutting down an atomic generating plant might protect, rather than harm, fish. Not so, unfortunately, in this case. The dead fish were discovered downstream the next day.

For two years, the Oyster Creek plant had drawn some 450,000 gallons of water per minute from Barnegat Bay to cool the steam created by the atomic reactor system. After being used as a coolant, the water was dumped back into Oyster Creek, a tributary of the bay.

But this recirculated water was now 15 to 20 *degrees F. hotter*. As a result, in the middle of winter, Oyster Creek became a warm, mild stream.

The dead fish found in Oyster Creek after the plant shut down were warm water species. Mossbunkers usually cannot stand the cold New Jersey waters and migrate south to the warmer waters off the North Carolina coast each winter.

Since the heated waters discharged by the atomic cooling system created spring-like temperatures in Oyster Creek all year long, the mossbunkers were unaware that the seasons were changing and they remained in the north after summer ended.

When the atomic plant shut down, the water temperature dropped suddenly by 22 degrees F. Overnight, the creek returned to its normal winter conditions.

Unprotected and unprepared for this rapid arrival of winter, the mossbunkers became the victims of "thermal shock." The sudden cold snap literally jolted their bodily functions to a standstill.

The Oyster Creek fish kill underlines still another danger associated with atomic energy plants. For many years, environmentalists have been concerned about the effects of heating on marine biology and plants. Not many people have considered the reverse situation: What happens when the unnatural heat supply is turned off? How many more fish will die after being fooled into thinking it is June in January?

THE DISAPPEARING PAVEMENT

Late one winter night in 1973, a young man and his date, both residents of Swansea, Wales, were driving home from a party at a friend's house. The night was clear and surprisingly mild for winter. The party had been fun, the food and drink delicious, and the couple were in fine spirits.

Then the road disappeared!

Suddenly a pleasant drive had turned into a nightmare. As the front end of the car lurched forward into apparent nothingness, the panic-stricken driver slammed on his brakes. The car skidded, its underframe scraped the ground, and then, miraculously, the back wheels caught on solid pavement. The car stopped with a sickening seesaw motion, its headlights pointing downward into a deep black chasm.

The couple sat stunned for several minutes. Terrified that any false move might send the car toppling into this bottomless pit, they edged toward the doors and carefully opened the latches. Then, together they jumped from the car and ran back down the road away from the gaping gulf.

Once calmed down, the couple ventured back to the car and the hole in the road to see what had happened. They found their car on the brink of a huge pit nearly 20 feet wide and 30 feet deep. They were baffled.

The police arrived shortly after and pulled the car from the edge of the hole, roping off a section of highway in case of further collapse. But they too were puzzled by this strange phenomenon. What had caused the pavement to disappear in Swansea?

The mystery was cleared up soon, with the arrival of geologists —and officials from the national mining commission. The pavement on the Swansea road didn't really disappear, it fell into an old air shaft that had ventilated a mine abandoned some fifty years before.

Local residents remembered that 16 years earlier a similar collapse had occurred a mile away. That collapse, too, had been into an old lost mine.

Swansea is undercut with miles and miles of unused coal mine tunnels. Many of these mines were closed so long ago that no one even knows where they led. As the modern city of Swansea developed, homes and roads and shopping centers have been built over these lost mines. Today, the entire city sits on a honeycombed substrata that seems ready to collapse at any moment.

It's possible that the rest of Swansea may one day suddenly disappear into a huge deep pit!

STRANGE TOURISTS

Japanese seaweed is bobbing in the surf off England. African fish are basking in the Florida sunshine. Tahitian beetles are bugging Samoa. And Chinese clams are clogging drains in Pennsylvania.

The Jet Set is not limited to human beings. Scores of exotic plants and animals are circling the globe—some carried as stowaways on planes and boats and others deliberately carted along in the baggage of unthinking tourists and well-meaning scientists.

Unfortunately, some of these foreign visitors find their new homes so pleasant that they have taken root—with disastrous results. Carried to an environment where they have no natural enemies or diseases, the strange tourists multiply at abnormal rates and crowd out the native stock.

For example, in 1973, British biologists found Japanese seaweed growing along their country's southern coastline.

Perhaps the seaweed arrived wrapped round the anchor chain of a Japanese ship. No one knows. But one thing is certain: the new breed of Oriental weed is crowding out the local species. Allowed to grow unchecked, it could change the ecology of the English coastal flats.

Similarly, a nasty little beetle has found its way to American Samoa aboard oil tankers sailing from Tahiti. Well known in other parts of the South Pacific, this beetle is a major destroyer of palm trees.

The beetle lays its eggs between the tightly rolled folds of sprouting leaves. When the eggs hatch, the beetle larvae (or worm stage) feed on the leaves, causing them to turn brown. Young palms that lose too many leaves soon wither and die.

In the American South, some popular pets have turned into ecological time bombs. Fresh-water species of imported tropical fish have found their way into Florida's inland lakes and rivers, dumped there from home aquariums or "fish farms."

A fish called the "black acara," for instance, has felt so at home that it now makes up 80 per cent of the population in many waterways. The "blue tilapia," an African version of the sunfish, was actually brought to Florida on purpose because scientists thought it would eat up harmful plant growth in the canals. The blue fish ate up the vegetation, all right, but it also drove out all the other native fish.

The Chinese clam is another foreign creature taking over American waters. No one knows how the Chinese clams arrived in the United States, but they were first spotted on the West Coast in 1938. (Maybe travellers from the Orient brought back a few as snacks and released them in rivers instead.) Now, thirty-five years later, the pesty clams have shown up in the East Coast rivers.

The small, grey, fresh-water bivalve multiplies at a phenomenal rate. Since it has no natural enemies, the population of clams in some areas has grown so large that they clog water valves and sewage drains, foul river beds, and crowd out other water life.

Actually, the clam problem could be solved—simply by eating them! The tiny shellfish is considered quite a delicacy in Asia; perhaps they will soon find a spot on American menus.

THE BOMBARDED WHALES

From the Bible to modern novels, the whale has served as the universal symbol of massive power, frightening strength, and monumental size.

Many scientists also think the great sea mammals—the whales and their cousins, the porpoises—may be the most intelligent non-human creatures alive. Indeed, some experts claim the minds of the whale and porpoise are more like that of man than any other animal.

Nothing, then, is more sad and sickening than to see these deep sea monarchs lying helpless and dying on a dry beach.

Yet, each year, the Smithsonian Center for Short-Lived Phenomena receives scores of reports of whales running aground on shallow sandbars and beaches to perish in the sun.

One of the strangest cases of beached whales was reported in February, 1971, when some three dozen giant sperm whales rammed themselves into the sand at Gunnamatta Beach near Melbourne, Australia.

The shocking picture of these animals spread out like some discarded black blimps produced outcries of dismay and anger, especially when the tragic reasons for the beaching became known.

Whales travel in herds, just like cattle, elephants, or tribes of men. Led by an old bull, or chief, they respond to group pressures and instincts.

Whales also communicate with each other, as well as navigate through the water, by means of a sophisticated natural sonar system. They send out high-pitched beeping noises that bounce off obstacles and objects underwater, such as reefs and sand shoals, to help them negotiate the murky depths. The system works best in deep water.

At Gunnamatta Beach this intricate sonar system may have been confused by something man did.

Two days before the whales were found on the beach, a naval installation about nine miles east of Gunnamatta held gunnery practice for several hours in the morning.

Scores of anti-aircraft practice shells were fired over the ocean to explode above the water's surface.

Since the shells didn't detonate in the water, it is unlikely that any of the whales were physically harmed. However, the air bursts might have caused shock waves damaging to their sonar systems.

Even more likely, the sound of the explosions may have so frightened the whales that they became panicky and confused. Losing their direction in the surf, the whales probably swam into the shallow waters near the coast by mistake. Once in shallow waters, their sonar would become totally useless. Perhaps they then rushed onto the beach in a suicidal frenzy to escape the sound of the explosions—and their own fright.

THE ELK CITY BOULDERS

"Galloping granite! Call the sheriff! The Fire Department and the National Guard, too! There's big boulders sprouting up in the back forty!"

The residents of Elk City, Oklahoma, surely were shocked in the spring of 1973 to see huge boulders suddenly pop out of the ground in the middle of Jim Walker's pasture.

The rocks, all red shale, tore through the bed of a small creek crossing Walker's ranch and created a natural version of Stonehenge: a wall-like formation of tall jagged stones, some standing 20 feet high and weighing as much as 30 tons.

In addition, a host of smaller boulders were strewn over an area 230 feet long and 100 feet wide. A network of deep narrow crevices spread outward from the rocks. Many trees and shrubs were uprooted and toppled by the force of the boulder upheaval.

Scientists from the Oklahoma Geological Survey arrived on the scene the next day. The puzzled experts attempted to explain why these mysterious monoliths were now jutting from the normally flat and gentle grazing land.

They ruled out the possibility of a giant meteorite impact, or of a volcanic eruption, or even of an earthquake along existing fault lines. Instead, the geologists felt the boulder uplift was probably caused by the non-explosive build-up of pressure from propane gas—the same gas used to heat homes.

Oklahoma is a major producer of fossil fuels, including oil and natural gas. In 1953, one of the large oil companies drilled a well just 2,000 feet north of the now boulder-strewn pasture. This well bottomed out at about 1,300 feet in a salt bed. The oil company then turned the dry shaft into an underground storage tank for liquid petroleum gas, or propane.

Apparently for the next ten years, propane gas had slowly leaked through the well-casing into the surrounding rocks. Finally the pressure became so great it caused expansion and uplifting of the shale levels.

Man's interference with Earth's natural order had resulted in an unusual and totally unexpected geological disturbance—causing Jim Walker's quiet pasture to be turned into a giant rock-pile.

MOTHS ON THE MOVE

Unbelievable sights are commonplace in the tropics. Nature seems to conjure up its wildest magic in the steamy regions around the Equator. Here the combination of intense sun and extreme moisture produces the biggest, brightest, and often most beautiful of nature's plants, animals, and insects. Yet even the long-time residents of the tropics are sometimes thrilled and surprised by one of nature's more spectacular shows.

For example, during one week in August 1969, the residents of Panama City were bedazzled by the appearance of millions of green and black "butterflies." The skies were literally filled throughout the day with these magnificent creatures as they migrated across the city.

According to scientists at the Smithsonian's Tropical Research Institute in the Canal Zone, these beautiful "butterflies" actually were moths. Known formally as the *Urania fulgens*, this moth is closely related to the well-known "Green Page" species found in Trinidad.

Some sort of moth migration occurs almost every year in Panama, with the insects moving west in the dry season and back east again in the rainy season.

The moth migration of 1969, therefore, was not unique. But few people could ever remember having seen so many of the "butterflies" before. Apparently, the previous year's weather had provided a particularly good breeding season. The multitude of moths was the product of a natural population explosion.

As far as biologists could determine, however, this was one population explosion that caused no one any grief. Just the opposite. The moths put on a great show for those people who just like to sit back and watch nature fly by.

The moths only flew during the day, so they were particularly visible. Apparently, they navigate by the sun, so the sky was dense with moths each dawn as huge flocks took off for their day's flight.

These moths are unusually strong fliers. They cruise along at a rate of about eight miles an hour, so they can cross Panama from

end to end in about a week. Moreover, they can cross mountains and even wide stretches of open sea with ease.

Because they are so strong, the moths easily avoid most dangerous obstacles, including collectors' nets. And they don't seem to have any natural enemies. Most birds don't even try to eat them.

If the moths faced any hazard on their journey across Panama, it was from man's own greatest menace in this modern age—the automobile! During the week of their migration, thousands (maybe millions) of moths met squishy deaths against windshields, headlights, and radiator grills.

But at least in death the moths had their revenge: Traffic was tied up all over Panama, as irate drivers were forced out of their cars to clean green and black wings from their windshields.

THE SLIDES OF DEATH

One minute Dr. Liu Chen was sitting in his luxurious apartment overlooking the lights of Hong Kong Bay, the next minute he was picking himself out of a pile of rubble. Surrounded by the wreckage of his home and office, with the painful sounds of the dying ringing in his ears, the doctor considered himself lucky just to be alive.

Not so lucky were the more than 100 people killed and the other thousands left injured and homeless by massive landslides down the hills of Hong Kong following three days of torrential rain in June 1973.

Hong Kong, a small, congested island, an outcropping of rock —just off the mainland of China, plus a peninsula connected only by a narrow neck—is one of the last British Crown Colonies: a strange outpost of capitalism surrounded by the Communist world. Because Hong Kong represents a freedom unknown in mainland China, its narrow streets are thronged with people, the island's steep hills are stacked with houses. Some of these houses are the fashionable and expensive homes of super-rich traders and merchants. More often, they are the shacks and shanties of the manual workers, office workers, street vendors, and impoverished refugees who continue to pour into this city-state. But rich or poor, death recognized no class barriers when tons of rock and mud went hurtling down the hillsides.

The disaster was touched off by unusual weather conditions. More than 25 inches of rain fell on the city in less than 3 days. Storm drains became thundering waterfalls, roadways turned into swollen rivers, and low-lying areas became flooded lakes. Communication, transportation, and power lines were cut throughout the city.

Under this constant battering, the overloaded slopes could hold no longer. In one of the worst slides, in the Kwuntong District, a huge section of hillside, 150 feet high and 600 feet wide, plummeted into a cluster of shanty-town huts housing some 400 people.

The other major landslide occurred in the more exclusive district of Victoria Peak, where apartment houses perch on rocky ledges above the port. Here, an apartment building near the top of the slope collapsed. As it fell, it smashed into a second structure which, in turn, hit a third and then a fourth. Like giant dominoes, the buildings toppled over in a horrible chain-reaction.

On the fourth day, the rains ended. But their toll was enormous. Since the destruction had cut across economic lines, both rich and poor mourned their losses.

THE BOILING LAKE

For most winter-weary North Americans, the blue Caribbean is a tropical playground of tiny islands where one finds the warmth of the sun. One of those islands, St. Vincent, is among the last green pearls on the long necklace that stretches south from Puerto Rico to Trinidad. St. Vincent is part of a lush world of quiet lagoons and beautiful beaches.

Towering over this peaceful Caribbean hideaway is the Soufriere Volcano. The 1902 eruption of Soufriere caused widespread destruction. Since then, the volcano has lain still. In fact, Soufriere has remained so inactive that a deep dark mountain lake formed in its crater.

But in the fall of 1971, people came down the mountains of St. Vincent with reports of strange things happening high in the Soufriere crater. The lake had changed color and some unknown and unseen turbulence was churning up the surface.

When scientists climbed to the crater rim, they found the surface of the lake half obscured by mists and vapors. Occasionally, an updraft lifted the warm and wettish vapors to the rim, engulfing the men in a foul-smelling mist.

There could be no mistake. A large heat source—most likely molten rock—had pushed up from the lake floor. Steam or hot lava blowing through the cracks in the lake bed was heating the water. Soufriere was showing the first signs of a major eruption!

Within the next few days, the scientists made the long descent into the crater. At the bottom, they found that the water level had recently risen, drowning the plants and smaller trees along the steep-sided shore. The water of the crater lake was warm to the touch, yellowish-brown to the eye, and sulphurous to the nose. While apparently smooth and calm, the entire surface seemed to be steaming—with vapor rising as steadily and as thick as one of the old-time London pea-soup fogs.

Most amazing, the scientists found a brand-new island sitting in the center of the lake! This island—made up of approximately a dozen large blocks of black rock—represented the topmost part of a dome-shaped lava mass that had been slowly seeping through the floor of the lake for more than a month.

In the next two months, this rocky island rose some 30 feet above the lake's surface, spreading 1,000 feet long and 300 feet wide.

Although the threat of a violent eruption remained very real, the absence of any unusual or strong earthquake activity greatly reduced the chances of a major disaster.

So confident of Soufriere's safety were two of the scientists that they rowed out into the middle of the steaming lake to plant an earthquake monitor on the island itself. As they neared the pile of hot rocks, they found the water getting progressively warmer. Indeed, at the very edge of the island, where water directly contacted the emerging lava, the lake was literally boiling! The scientists dropped off their instruments and rowed quickly back to the crater rim.

The Soufriere crater bubbled for a few months more and then returned to its usual dormant state. St. Vincent had been spared a repeat of the terrible 1902 eruption. Of course, now this little island in the sun has its own little island nestling in the mouth of the Soufriere Volcano.

PESTY PARAKEETS

The New York businessman gazed out of his office window and saw a sight he could hardly believe. In the middle of winter, there on the window ledge, 20 floors above Fifth Avenue sat a small grey parrot!

The monk parakeet, a tropical native, has found a new home in North America. Worse yet, this one-time harmless household pet for thousands of Americans has turned into a major pest that threatens to upset the already delicate ecology balance of the urbanized East Coast.

This chattering little bird, with its grey plumage vaguely

resembling a friar's hood, has long been the scourge of farmers throughout South America. Yet, despite its bad reputation, more than 50,000 birds were imported into the United States as pets between 1968 and 1972.

Some of these birds escaped or were released, and now small parakeet colonies have become established in New York, New Jersey, and Connecticut. And sightings of the monk parakeets have been reported from over 20 other states, ranging from North Dakota to Arizona.

Several hundred of the birds are estimated to be living wild in New York City alone. Although usually found in subtropical regions of South America, the birds can apparently survive winter temperatures as low as zero degrees F. by building nests in the warm sheltered nooks and crannies provided by a modern city.

Flocks of birds in the countryside may also build large communal nests of sticks in which they live. Most of the nest sites are built close to fruit trees, such as wild cherry, apple and mulberry. The nests themselves are built from the twigs of these trees and are woven together to produce a large dwelling with one or more entrance tunnels located on the lower side of the nest.

Usually the nests are built in the eaves of buildings, or on telephone poles and trees between 20 and 30 feet from the ground. These nests are often located on a hill or in an open area where the birds can observe approaching danger.

No monk parakeets have been imported to the United States since 1972 when the Department of Agriculture placed a ban on them.

Some experts think this ban may cause the decline of the birds; but others are not so optimistic. No natural diseases or parasites seem to affect the birds in North America.

In their native habitat of Argentina, Bolivia, Brazil, Uruguay, and Paraguay, the parakeets are major agricultural pests, destroying thousands of dollars worth of corn, millet, sorghum, and other grains, as well as citrus fruits each year. Worse news: The Argentine government has tried to wipe out the birds since 1947 —by every means possible—and nothing yet has worked!

THE ROCK IN THE ROOF

Just before dawn on April 8, 1971, an early-rising resident of West Hartford, Connecticut, looked out of her window and saw "a bright streak of light like a rocket bursting in the air!" A long dark trail like that from a jet aircraft remained above the horizon for several minutes.

About an hour later, the alarm rang in the home of Paul Cassarino in nearby Wethersfield. Mr. Cassarino, who was a machinist at America's last horseshoe nail factory, awakened and walked from the bedroom into the living room of his second-floor apartment. He immediately noticed something odd. A small pile of plaster and dust lay in the middle of the carpet.

Angered because he had just paid to have his ceiling plastered, he looked up to see what had happened to the new work.

His mouth dropped open with surprise and he nearly toppled over backwards.

There, poking out of the middle of his smooth white plastered ceiling, was a small black rock.

Mr. Cassarino climbed onto an armchair and with the blade of his penknife pried the stone loose. It was about 3 inches in diameter and unusually heavy. By squinting up through the hole in the plaster, he could see there was also a hole in the fiberglass insulation material between the ceiling eaves, and still another hole through the boards and asbestos tiles of the roof itself.

Whatever this strange object was—it had fallen out of the sky! Mr. Cassarino called the police.

The police—plus the fire department and several assorted reporters—arrived at his home almost immediately. Not one of them could offer a reasonable explanation for the rock that had torn through his roof. Luckily, someone else also heard about this strange event: a local astronomer, who stopped by that same morning to survey the stone.

The astronomer's answer was fast and to the point! Mr. Cassarino's house had been hit by a meteorite—a piece of outer space material that had entered the atmosphere and crashed through the roof with the last remaining force of its fall. It was probably the same object that had been seen over Hartford as a "bursting rocket" earlier that morning.

The 12.3-ounce stone, now known as the Wethersfield Meteorite, was only the eleventh in the past century known to have struck a building.

Luckily, scientists anxious to receive samples of the meteorite for analysis and study provided Mr. Cassarino with enough money to fix his roof.

WHERE HAVE ALL THE PUFFINS GONE?

The puffin, a large, rotund, diving bird that paddles about the cold northern Atlantic seas, seems doomed to the same fate as the dodo—*extinction!*

Reports from professional and amateur bird-watchers in the Hebrides Islands near the west coast of Scotland indicate the puffin population is rapidly and mysteriously declining.

At one time, millions upon millions of puffins—the smallest member of the auk family and a northern version of the penguin —ranged the waters from Brittany to Norway. Even as late as

1960, some 3 million pairs of puffins roosted in the craggy rock islands jutting from the sea west of Scotland.

Ten years ago the mile-long island of Dun was riddled with puffin burrows, or nests. But by 1969, only half the island was covered with nesting birds.

Then, in 1972, a bird census by British officials indicated that Dun's puffin population, once numbered in the millions, had now been reduced to about 250,000 birds.

The cause of this rapid puffin decline is a mystery. All possible reasons have been investigated—attacks by rats, seagulls, and man; food shortages; breeding failures; epidemic disease; even oil pollution—but none are likely killers. However, in winter, the puffins migrate to distant and little-watched waters where they may be tangling with other poisonous materials dumped in the water by man.

Professional bird-watchers urge that world-wide efforts be made to investigate the puffin decline and its possible causes. If the answers aren't found soon, they fear the puffin may join the long and tragic list of extinct birds.

Some 161 species of birds have disappeared since 1600, with 54 species lost in the 20th century alone. Most of these missing birds, such as the American passenger pigeon and the heath hen, have been the victims of man.

The classic victim was the dodo, a big, lovable bird that could neither fly nor swim and died because of its trusting nature.

The dodo lived on the island of Mauritius in the Indian Ocean. With only rudimentary wings and no swimming ability, the two-foot-tall dodo apparently came to the island aboard logs that had drifted out to sea. On Mauritius, without any natural enemies or disease, dodos multiplied and prospered until the first explorers arrived in the early 1600's.

Gentle, curious, and trusting, the dodos waddled down to the beach to look at the strange two-legged creatures and were immediately clubbed over the head and either roasted for dinner or cut up as fish bait. (The apparent willingness of the dodo to submit to its own slaughter gave rise to the phrase "dumb as a dodo.")

Those dodos that somehow escaped the cooking pots soon fell

victim to the many diseases brought ashore by the sheep, goats, and rats carried on the visiting ships. Long-removed from the mainland, the dodos had lost any natural immunity to the diseases of the outside world. The last dodo on earth died in 1681.

The puffin at least can fly—in a sense, anyhow. Although smaller than the dodo, the puffin shares certain features with its extinct cousins—an oversized body and undersized wings. In fact, the puffin is so disproportionately built, it cannot take off from a standing start. Instead, the clumsy bird must launch itself by jumping from a high rock or cliff.

While this lumbering flight allows the puffin to escape enemies such as seagulls, rats, and men, some other still unknown and deadly form of killer is reducing the puffin flocks. The number of newly hatched puffins—little round fluffy balls that resemble chirping cream puffs—is declining yearly. Unless someone can discover—and stop—the cause of their decline, the puffin may join the dodo. Gone forever!

KRAKATOA MAY STRIKE AGAIN

When the volcano Krakatoa blows its top, the whole world seems to hear about it. The small volcanic island in the Sunda Strait between Sumatra and Java, erupted in August 1883 with the greatest natural display of raw power and destructive fury ever recorded in modern history.

The tremendous force of the volcanic eruption completely disintegrated most of the island and permanently altered the shape of the strait. As the old volcanic cone split apart, red-hot lava and incandescent boulders poured into the surrounding waters and turned the sea into a boiling, bubbling broth.

A large portion of the sea floor collapsed creating a series of towering tidal waves that capsized boats of every size and description and flooded low coastal areas in minutes, killing thousands of sailors, fishermen, and their families.

The sound of the explosion, perhaps the loudest noise ever heard, resounded throughout Indonesia, the Philippines, Australia and, unbelieveably, as far away as Japan, 3,000 miles distant.

The volume of ash and smoke released by Krakatoa was so great that the sky turned black at mid-day and hunks of volcanic debris were scattered across the Indian Ocean as far as Madagascar, 4,000 miles away.

One massive cloud of dust particles was carried high into the upper atmosphere and circled the earth three times, creating brilliant sunsets in Europe and North America for more than a year after the eruption.

While nothing could compare with the dramatic and devastating events of 1883, Krakatoa erupted again in 1972. And, again, much of the world felt the after-effects.

On April 11, a crewman on a Scottish freighter bound for Djakarta spotted what seemed to be extremely high waves breaking against the southern shore of Krakatoa. Closer inspection revealed that an underwater eruption was churning up the coastal waters into a turbulent, steamy froth.

Thin lines of smoke seeped from cracks in the mountainside near the old volcanic peak, and a spray of fine white ash had settled over the southwestern side of the mountain.

Throughout the next few months, similar activity could be observed at Krakatoa. Thunder-like rumblings could be heard and puffs of dirty-white ash rose high in the air. At night, angry red streaks of flame shot through the murky clouds of smoke and dust.

In early September, weather observers on islands throughout the Western Pacific reported unusually high levels of smoke and haze that persisted for many days. In both the Caroline and Marshall Islands, 2,500 miles to the northeast, visibility was down to three miles—extremely poor conditions for lands traditionally sunny and clear.

The darkening clouds drifted over the Pacific on southwesterly breezes, indicating to many meteorologists that the strange source of pollution in paradise must have been that old scourge of the Sunda Strait again—the Krakatoa volcano!

THE SUPERBEES OF BRAZIL

Hide your honey pots! Lock your doors and close your windows! Get out the leather gloves and protective goggles! The Brazilian superbees are headed north!

Professional beekeepers and scientists from several Western Hemisphere countries are bracing for the most fantastic and potentially dangerous invasion of insects in the 20th century.

A line of defense is being established at the Panama Canal to stop the northward drive of millions of mean and nasty big superbees from Brazil.

The superbees are mutants: the unnatural and unwanted products of an ill-fated and unwise attempt to improve South American honeybees.

In the late 1950's, some South American farmers imported a strain of African bees in order to develop a stronger and more productive species for the local honey industry. Unfortunately, about two dozen of these bees—with their queens—escaped from the experimental breeding station and flew off into the jungles of Southern Brazil.

For the next decade, unnoticed and unchecked in the wild, these African bees interbred with the European-type bees then found in Brazil. The result has been a new race of superbees: strong and productive, but also unpredictable, unmanageable, aggressive, and blood-thirsty. Indeed, huge swarms of "Brazilian bees" have been known to attack men and animals without warning or provocation. In some cases, the attacks have been fatal.

The new breed of bee is apparently replacing the milder and more manageable honeybees. Worse yet, they seem to be spreading steadily over South America—and have already crossed the natural barrier of the Amazon River. Based on their current rate of spread, this means they should reach Panama before 1980. From there, it's only a short flight to the United States, where experts suspect they could survive as far north as Virginia. Indeed, there is no known geological or climate barrier that could stop the spread of bees in North America.

An international committee has been formed to find ways of halting this northward advance of bees in Central America. Most scientists hope to modify or improve the superbee breed so its strength and honey production can be preserved—but its nastiness eliminated!

THE KILLER WHALES ATTACK!

For centuries, fishermen have told tales of fantastic battles between deadly killer whales and giant elephant seals. But were these stories true? No one had ever witnessed and confirmed such attacks. Some people claimed they were only myths, similar to the tales of sea serpents and mermaids.

The legend became real life, however, in December 1973, when two American naturalists had front-row seats for a frightening show: the attack and killing of a two-ton elephant seal by two blood-thirsty killer whales.

The two men were floating in a small boat off the coast of Mexico's Baja California Peninsula on a bright, sunny afternoon, photographing and recording the hunting and feeding behavior of killer whales.

Suddenly, they noticed a commotion near the shoreline. Two killer whales, one a 20-foot male, the other a 15-foot female, were apparently stalking a huge bull elephant seal.

Like cowboys with a stray steer, the whales circled the clumsy seal, lunging and pushing at it, their jaws snapping, so that the animal was driven from its relatively safe haven in the shallow coastal waters. Slowly, surely, deliberately, the two whales, working as a team, pushed the seal toward open sea and its doom.

Once in deeper waters, the seal was at the mercy of the whales. In a flash, they began their attack.

The bull whale charged the seal and slashed at its soft under-belly. The huge seal bellowed in pain and beat at the water with its ineffectual flippers. Around the wounded animal, the frothing sea quickly turned pink.

While the cow whale waited a distance away, as if blocking any avenue of escape, the bull whale attacked a second time. Again, the seal was viciously cut.

Still once more the whale attacked. This time, the result was fatal. The mammoth elephant seal, perhaps once a proud and strong leader of a herd, disappeared beneath the waters. The entire attack had taken just a few minutes. Only blood and some tufts of fur remained floating on the surface above the battle zone.

The two naturalists sat stunned in their small skiff. The horrifying battle had taken place before their eyes, without any of the animals paying the slightest attention to them.

Perhaps the most chilling part of the battle was its aftermath: The killer whales simply turned from their stricken foe and swam away! They made no attempt to feed on their victim. They had killed out of hate, not hunger. Until the next time, at least, the whales ruled this part of the sea.

FIRE IN THE LAKE

The Great Rift Valley slices through East Africa like the track of a giant's plow.

Beginning in the Gulf of Aden, the Rift runs inland, splitting the lowlands of the Somalia Peninsula from the Ethiopian highlands, then turns west and south to create the chain of mountain lakes—Rudolf, Dwania, Albert, Tanganyika, and Nyasa—that feed the Nile and Congo Rivers.

For geologists, the Rift represents a major seam in the armorplate crust of the Earth. Along this seam, they say, the continent of Africa may be splitting apart, with its two halves drifting off in opposite directions.

While the actual separation of the African continent is still some eons away, the Rift has created a fantastic landscape of towering cliffs, yawning chasms, fathomless lakes, cascading waterfalls, and spectacular volcanoes.

One of the most spectacular of these is also one of the rarest and most unusual types in the world. Nyrangongo is a vast bubbling lake of red-hot lava deep inside a high mountain crater.

Nyrangongo is located north of Lake Kivu in the volcanic range of the Virunga Mountains marking the boundary between Zaïre and the African nations of Uganda and tiny Rwanda.

For more than forty years, this lake of glowing, steaming molten lava has been almost constantly active. Loss of heat at the surface of the lake produces a dark sluggish crust, but the seething molten mass below constantly cracks this ash-like covering so that bright crimson steaks of liquid lava show through.

Nyrangongo is particularly striking at night, when the deep bowl-like crater looks like a devil's cauldron of some fiendish brew.

When the volcano was first discovered 75 years ago this lava lake was not visible, for the inside of the crater was ringed by a series of overhanging ledges or rims apparently marking the various lava levels of past eruptions.

Even in 1928, when scientists first began systematic surveys of the volcano, no lake could be seen from the wall of the main crater because the lava lay beneath three interior ledges. A bright red glow at night from the bowels of the mountain gave unmistakable evidence of its presence, however.

But the nature of Nyrangongo has changed dramatically in the past 20 years, particularly, since 1965, when the lava lake changed from a tiny molten pool deep at the crater bottom to the present vast lake covered with a cool crust.

The lava lake is still rising steadily and rapidly—sometimes as much as several feet in a few hours.

Most interesting, perhaps, the lake now seems to grow by

lava from below forcing its way through fissures and cracks in the crust to cool on top.

Before the crust formed in 1965, the entire column of lava seemed to rise and fall together, pushed up from below. Now, in a manner of speaking, the lake is growing from the top down.

Various expeditions visit Nyrangongo each year to study the phenomenon first hand. Volcanic activity permitting, some scientists actually camp inside the main crater on a natural platform only 700 feet above the boiling lava.

For several weeks at a time, these researchers make extensive temperature, pressure, and heat measurements as part of the plan to chart Nyrangongo's long-term ups and downs.

The goal of this and other research efforts at this fantastic volcano is to develop a better understanding of volcanic activity, so that some day in the future man may be able to predict more accurately the next time a mountain will blow its top.

THE POISONED SHEEP

Even the crusty old shepherd nearly broke into tears when he looked at the hillside. Strewn among the rock and sagebrush, in all directions as far as the eye could see, lay countless small white clumps of wool. Half his herd of sheep were dead—victims of a mysterious and silent killer.

When more than 1,250 sheep were found dead in a mountain pasture near Garrison, Utah, in 1972, the immediate reaction of most local residents was stark fear. Garrison is downwind from the U.S. Army's Dugway Proving Ground, where the newest and most deadly kinds of poison gas are developed and tested.

Could the sheep have been killed by nerve gas escaping from these test laboratories? And, worse yet, would the residents of Garrison be the next victims?

Perhaps the fears of Garrison were justified. Scattered cases of death and sickness caused by spills of bacteriological and radioactive materials have been only too well known in the last thirty years in the U.S.

This time, however, Garrison—and all America—would be lucky. The sheep were not gassed by a new secret weapon—they had been killed by one of nature's own equally lethal and secretive poisons.

Unknowingly, the sheep had fed on a toxic weed known as *halogeton*. This low, red, prickly plant contains unusual amounts of moisture, and so is particularly attractive to sheep. Unfortunately, it is also deadly! In the digestive system of the sheep, the weed turns into fast-acting poison. (Ironically, cattle can eat the same weed without any ill effects.)

Half the herd had apparently wandered into a section of range where this killer weed made up some 60 per cent of the vegetation. The other half of the herd grazed on a different hillside less than a mile away and survived.

Indeed, it was the survival of the other sheep that made investigators doubt poison gas as a cause of death. The gas would have killed every living creature in its path—including the people of Garrison—if it had escaped.

VIOLENT BIRTH

Karua, one of the South Pacific's newest islands, is growing into a healthy young adult and scientists around the world are relieved to find their baby is living so long.

The tiny world of Karua was born in a spasm of volcanic violence; and, like any proud and worried parents, marine biologists and volcanologists waited apprehensively to see if this new addition would survive the terrible pains of its delivery.

On February 22, 1971, the submarine volcano Karua blasted up from the sea floor less than five miles from the island called Epi in the New Hebrides archipelago northeast of Australia.

Throughout most of that first day, the sea bubbled and churned around Karua as ashes spewed from beneath the sea. A cloud of smoke rose more than 3,000 feet over the volcano. Several times each minute, explosions shattered the quiet of the blue Pacific and hurled massive boulders high in the air.

The following morning, after the smoke and dust and steam had cleared away, scientists on nearby islands could see waves lapping against a black cinder pile nearly 600 feet long, 200 feet wide and several feet high.

Two days later, a small group of adventurous scientists took a motor launch out to the still warm island. The strange black, barren landscape, dotted with craters and cracked with volcanic vents, looked like a section of the moon.

In most scientific catalogs, Karua was listed only as a "volcanic area." Under normal conditions, the cone of Karua lay submerged and dormant beneath the surface, its location marked only by a lighter shade of ocean blue.

Yet, twice before in recent history—once at the turn of the century and again in the late 1940's—Karua had erupted and created similar islands. In 1901, it produced an island almost a mile long. In 1948, a volcanic cone over a mile in diameter protruded some 300 feet from the ocean. Neither island lasted more than a year.

The lava usually produced by oceanic volcanoes is a frothy, porous, and extremely fragile material—certainly not suited to withstand the battering of waves or even the constant flow of gentle currents.

Three years before, a similar island had bubbled out of the sea after a volcanic eruption several hundred miles east of Karua.

At first, the pilot of the island-hopping airliner on route to Fiji from Tonga thought a ship was in trouble. He banked his plane sharply toward the faint plume of smoke rising off his starboard wing.

As he flew nearer the coral shallows known as Metis Shoals, he quickly realized this was no shipwreck.

A thick grey column of smoke billowed more than 3,000 feet in the air—straight out of the water.

Around the base of the smoke column, the sea bubbled and boiled. And just beneath the surface, Metis Shoals glowed cherry-red.

A new volcano was being born before his eyes.

The Metis Shoals eruption soon became the most exciting event of the year for the islanders of the South Pacific. Journalists from as far away as New Zealand flew out to take pictures. Even the King of Tonga chartered a plane for a closer look.

The incredible sight was well worth the trip. The undersea volcano created a kidney-shaped island more than a half-mile long and 150 feet high. Curiosity seekers kept their distance, however, for huge molten boulders shot more than 1,000 feet out of the sea about once a minute.

By the time news of the volcano reached the United States, the eruptions had stopped and waves lapped over the new and now quiet island.

Unfortunately, the eruption produced a very fragile and frothy type of pumice stone that could not withstand the constant beating of the waves. Metis Shoals might soon disappear without a trace.

At that time, a Smithsonian scientist, Dr. Charles Lundquist, travelling to Australia, took a quick detour to investigate Metis Shoals before it disappeared. He chartered a rusty old cargo ship to take him and two native divers out to the vanishing island.

His little makeshift expedition arrived at the shoals just in time. Already, the fragile peaks of Metis Shoals had washed away and only a few jagged points of rock poked above the surface.

While the ship circled at a safe distance, the two divers paddled out to the island and dove down to break a half-dozen basket-ball-sized pieces of lava from its submerged shores.

Shortly after Dr. Lundquist left Tonga, the island sank back into the sea. Today, at the Smithsonian in Washington, only those crumbly bits of grey rock remain to prove that Metis Shoals ever existed.

Fortunately, scientists now have more than that to show from Karua! The bleak little lava pile seems determined to remain alive and well above the waters.

Given enough time and the right conditions, windblown seeds and spores could take root on Karua and create a full-fledged, permanent member of the New Hebrides island chain.

THE SAD SAGA OF SUZIE

For nearly a month and a half in the summer of 1973, whale lovers around the world rooted for Suzie, the sole survivor of a beaching incident that killed eight other members of her herd.

On June 13th, nine pilot whales stranded themselves on Grassy Key, about seven miles northeast of Marathon, Florida. Eight were dead. But one whale—a 6-foot-long, 500-pound young female—was found alive, floundering in shallow waters offshore, by members of the Florida Marine Patrol.

Repeated efforts to tow the surviving whale into deep water were unsuccessful. She seemed determined to head back onto the beach and die with her companions. In desperation, the men finally towed the young whale to a nearby boat basin where she was found to have serious sunburns covering her entire back. She was immediately coated with lanolin to reduce blistering and fed antibiotics to prevent infection.

Six days later, this whale—by now dubbed "Suzie" by her many new friends—was moved to the Flipper Sea School at Marathon. Here she was treated by a veterinarian and tube-fed a diet of minced fish and shrimp bolstered with vitamins and antibiotics. Within a week, her burns closed and healed without any infection and Suzie seemed to be in good physical condition.

Throughout the next month, marine biologists carefully watched Suzie's recovery. The rest of the world watched as well, for Suzie was setting new records for survival in captivity.

Pilot whales are also called "Atlantic blackfish," and males may grow to a length of 18 feet. The species is well known in East Coast waters, particularly for its strange and unexplained tendency to ram themselves onto beaches. Unfortunately, the skin of the pilot whale is particularly sensitive to the sun and quickly blisters when out of water. Also, they are unable to get rid of body heat effectively (they can't perspire like human beings), so beached whales die rapidly. None has ever survived for more than a few days after being rescued.

For a while, it seemed Suzie might be the exception. But then, in July, 45 days after she had been rescued from the shallow waters of Grassy Key, Suzie died.

For three days before her death she did not accept her special food and medicine mixture. Still, she did not appear to be suffering. In fact, Suzie had played actively in the large natural pool at the Flipper Sea School and fed on live snapper until the night before her death.

An autopsy indicated Suzie had died from a severe case of pneumonia that had been unnoticed by her helpers. Without her daily supply of antibiotics, her unsuspected lung condition had worsened and finally caused her death.

Ironically, Suzie was found in the shallowest end of the pool. As death approached, she apparently tried "to beach" herself again.

THE SLIPPING EARTH

Thousands of years ago, before even the native American Indian crossed the continent, vast areas of Quebec were covered by the waters of a great inland sea that now has shrunk to become Lake Champlain. As those waters evaporated and the sea dried up, a deep layer of soft clay was left in its place.

This clay was a very unstable material, about the same composition as the fine soft silt found on today's ocean floors. In fact, when exposed to water again, this clay would quickly liquefy and return to its original gummy, mucky state.

Nine thousand years later, man built a vast housing development on that clay base. Row after row of small white one-storey ranch-type houses lined perfectly straight and parallel streets above the ancient sea bed.

Of course, few residents of the modern town of St. Jean-Vianney, Quebec, knew the ancient history of their town. And none could have guessed they would one day be victims of geological processes that had begun eons earlier.

The spring of 1971 in Quebec had been unusually long and wet. Heavy winter snows had led to equally heavy spring run-offs from the rivers and streams of Canada's northern woods. The Petit Bras River that flowed past the town was running high and fast and a number of small landslips had occurred along its banks for several weeks in April.

Then late on the morning of May 4, while most housewives in St. Jean-Vianney were sitting down with a second cup of coffee, the bottom fell out of their town—and their lives!

Houses, cars, toys, playgrounds, gardens, garages, pets, and people suddenly dropped into a muddy wet pit: whirling, spinning, and turning in the debris; tumbling and churning with rocks, trees, and sections of lawn. The horrible sounds of wood splintering and stones crushing were mingled with the terrified cries of mothers and children caught in the horrible downward plunge.

Then all was silent.

A huge, 350,000-square-yard, section of St. Jean-Vianney had dropped 100 feet and then slid nearly a half-mile down a slope and into the Petit Bras River. Over 50 houses were destroyed. More than 40 people were killed, scores more were injured seriously.

The ancient inland sea—dry for centuries before any man ever trod its shores—had returned to its original slippery, unstable state. Some 9,000 years after it had evaporated and dried up, it was still claiming victims!

THE SURVIVORS

In an age of endangered species, hatch failures, and fish kills, isn't it nice to know that some species are surviving—and even thriving?

For example, 1973 was a banner year for butterflies. Throughout the autumn, East Coast residents of the U.S. watched seemingly endless streams of Monarch butterflies winging south. This peak year in the complex cycle of butterfly reproduction provided a rare thrill for butterfly collectors.

An even rarer phenomenon occurred in the preceding spring, when millions of "Painted Lady" butterflies were observed over Colorado. For several days, the skies over Denver were filled with butterflies circling aimlessly without any sense of direction. Then, one morning, as if on signal, the entire colorful flotilla flew off together northward.

Not all insect outbreaks are as beautiful as butterfly migrations, however. The Northeastern United States continue to be plagued by hordes of the forest-destroying Gypsy Moths. Also, millions of odd-looking insects known as "walking sticks" infest the Knobley Mountains of West Virginia defoliating vast areas of black locust and hackberry trees. And Massachusetts was recently visited by the hemlock looper, a hungry inchworm which chewed up acres of forest north of Boston.

Across the ocean in Belgium, oak, buckthorn, and hawthorn, along with many apple and pear trees, were stripped of their leaves and fruits by an army of brown-tail caterpillars. Although each caterpillar is only slightly longer than an inch, a colony of thousands can strip an entire tree bare of foliage overnight.

The Belgian caterpillar outbreak ended on a happy note, however. The bugs provided food for flocks of birds, especially the European cuckoo.

A squiggly, wiggly horde of hungry army worms ate its way

from southern Kenya into northern Tanzania during early 1971, destroying grassy pastures and valuable fields of maize, sorghum, and rice as it moved south.

The army worm actually is the yellow-grey larva of a moth known to gardeners almost everywhere as a *giant pest!* In its worm, or caterpillar, stage, the insect travels in large bands, feasts on green plants, and generally makes life miserable for farmers.

Although army worm "invasions," or, more precisely, infestations, occur annually in East Africa between November and May, this was one of the worst.

The army worms chewed up grasses and grains all along the

Kenya-Tanzania border, from Kilimanjaro to Karatu. Scattered outbreaks even threatened plant life in the world-famous Serengeti National Park. Rice and sorghum fields attacked by the worms were totally destroyed.

By lucky chance, many farmers had not yet planted their crops at the time of the worm invasion, and thus were spared from almost certain ruin. Still, almost 10,000 square miles were infested, with the insects numbering in the many, many millions! In some areas of the country observers counted more than 100 worms per square foot!

Fortunately, the voracious caterpillars were confined to the grazing pastures of the northern borders. However, new outbreaks usually followed the migratory paths of the adult moth, springing up later in the places where eggs are dropped.

To brace for future onslaughts of this strange army that literally travels on its stomach, East African officials now maintain special "worm watches," so counterattacks can be launched immediately against new outbreaks of the pest. Long-range "worm warnings" are issued to edgy farmers armed with pesticides. If the worms can be stopped before they mature as moths and reproduce again, major disasters—and possible famines—may be averted.

Apparent disasters sometimes do produce unexpected and beneficial side effects. The severe Mississippi floods of 1973 destroyed millions of dollars of property, but they also produced a bumper crop of red crayfish.

Crayfish are able to survive long periods of drought and extremely cold temperatures by "hibernating" in sealed burrows under the mud. The flood apparently awakened those crayfish lying dormant since the last high water.

Crayfish, which taste like shrimp, are important ingredients in such popular Creole dishes as jambalaya and "crawfish pie." But the little crustaceans are also a delicacy for many fish, birds, and bullfrogs living in the Mississippi Basin. In fact, the unexpected abundance of crayfish after the flood may have helped thousands of raccoons trapped on islands by high water to survive starvation.

Finally, the most positive note on the survival of the species came from the tiny Penikese Island off the coast of Massachusetts. In the spring of 1973, the Audubon Society spotted a pair of Manx shearwaters, members of the puffin family, nesting there.

Although the Manx shearwaters are great long-distance wanderers over the Atlantic, they normally nest in Europe and this was the first recorded nesting on the North American continent.

More important, the nest's single egg hatched successfully, thus marking the first known birth of such a bird in the United States.

Could this be the start of another population explosion?

THE ANTELOPE INVASION

Sometimes man may be a little too protective.

Ten years ago, the Saiga Antelope, a deer native to Kazakhstan in central Russia, was reported on the verge of extinction. Russian environmentalists immediately adopted restrictions against hunting them, designed to save the antelope.

So successful was this protection plan, that by 1965, the number of antelopes had been restored to a half-million. Unfortunately, that population continued to grow and grow . . . and grow! By 1971, it had risen to *one million* and was expected to double again in two years.

In such great numbers, the once threatened species quickly turned into a tremendous pest.

The largest herd of antelope—some 800,000 strong—winter in the remote desert country of Bet Pak Dala far to the south of Kazakhstan. Great numbers of the animals usually die each winter from heavy snows and cold. Thousands survive, however, to migrate northward in the spring away from the killing heat and dryness of the desert summer.

Recently, however, the old migration patterns have changed. Instead of heading for their usual summer pastures, the antelopes turn to the wheat fields of central Russia where they feast on the young shoots of the growing plants.

In addition to destroying these crops, the antelopes also carry diseases that can infect domestic cattle and horses.

Soviet officials are experimenting with many techniques for protecting both the wheat and the antelopes. For example, efforts have been made to drive off the antelopes by buzzing them with low-flying aircraft. Unfortunately, the deer tend to return to the wheat fields as soon as the planes leave.

Some environmentalists have suggested fencing off food areas along the migration routes so that the deer may have enough to eat without relying on the wheat. Alas, this plan seems much too expensive.

64

In the end, there may be a return to old practices that once nearly wiped out the antelopes. Russian farmers are hoping for a relaxation of the game laws so hunters can once again kill off the animals as they enjoy a long-time hunting sport.

STONE AGE MEETS SPACE AGE

While American astronauts toured the lunar landscape in their own "space sports car" during the summer of 1971, a team of scientists in the Philippine Islands discovered a forgotten tribe of primitive people who had never seen an ocean, never tasted salt, rice, or sugar, and who had never even heard of tobacco *let alone astronauts!*

First contact between the civilized world and the lost Tasaday people came on June 7, 1971, when a helicopter carrying an ex-

ploration team from the Philippine National Museum touched down in a small clearing high on a forested mountainside on rugged Mindanao Island.

Led into the forest by a native trader named Dafal, the anthropologists found a tiny band of 24 people who survived solely by trapping small animals and gathering wild plants and fruits.

The Tasaday had no knowledge of rice, sweet potatoes, corn, cassava, or any other cultivated plant. Indeed, they didn't even have words in their language for this type of food!

They had never tasted salt and sugar or smoked tobacco. (At first, the tribe refused gifts of salt and sugar, thinking them poisonous, but the small children quickly developed a taste for candy. No one, however, could be persuaded to smoke!)

The Tasadays still used stone tools—mainly flat, sharp rocks used as simple scrapers to make pointed bamboo spears and knives. Only four metal tools were found among the Tasadays, and all these had been given to them by the trader Dafal during the past five years.

Living in almost total social and geographical isolation, the Tasadays apparently had no formal trade or any contacts with anyone from the outside world except Dafal. Still, they seemed to know that other people lived around them, sometimes hearing the voices of hunters in the forest. A few of the braver Tasadays had even seen the fields and houses of the "strange people" who lived in the lowlands "near where the sun sets." Yet, the Tasadays had no words to describe or name other people and their own language seemed only loosely related to other Philippine tongues.

The entire world of the Tasadays was enclosed within the dense cloud-shrouded mountain forests where they are born, live, and die. Because their universe exists under these trees, they have no words for lakes, oceans, open fields, constellations or phases of the moon.

In fact, for the Tasadays, "heaven" existed in the tops of the trees. It was there that they went after death; and their ancestors "watched" them from the upper branches.

Rumors of these lost people had filtered down from other tribes living on the edges of the thick mountain forests. Members of the Manubo Blit tribe who hunt wild boar and deer with bow-and-arrow traps told of seeing an unknown people in the forest and finding camp sites where animals had been butchered.

It was one of these native trappers—Dafal—who first met the Tasadays. When he found them, by accident, they had no cloth, no metal tools, and not even a bow and arrow. Their only garments were large orchid leaves or strips of beaten tree bark tied about their waists with string.

Over several years of visiting the Tasadays, Dafal brought them metal bolo knives, cloth, bows, and a few feet of brass wire from which they made earrings.

The Tasadays live amidst some of the most isolated and rugged land in the Philippine Archipelago, yet only a 30-minute helicopter ride from a fairly large development at Kemato. The tribe lives along the headwaters of scores of small rivers and streams that begin high in the mountains and cut narrow twisting lanes through hundreds of miles of dark, damp forests.

The land, as hostile and inhospitable as it looks, has resources so limited that only a small number of Tasadays can be supported. Probably no more than 100 Tasadays exist in several small, loosely related, and widely scattered "bands," or family groups.

The basic diet of these people consists of wild yams and fruits, as well as some crabs, fish, and large tadpoles found in the streams.

If life is hard for the Tasadays, it is also short. The scientists found no elderly men and women among the group they met. Sickness, especially the type of disease brought in from the outside, wipes out the old and weak quickly.

In fact, when asked what they feared most, the Tasadays didn't say evil spirits, or wild animals, or other tribes, or even the strange aircraft that they must see flying over their forest homes. The most dreaded thing in their lives is *fugu*—epidemic sickness. With good reason! A disease like cholera—or even influenza—could destroy the Tasadays overnight, for they have no natural resistance to the germs of civilization.

This fear of disease—and the unconscious knowledge that it comes from outside—has made the Tasadays hide away from the world for centuries.

68

The Tasadays could not have hid much longer. Their forest home is being rapidly invaded by homesteading farmers, loggers, and ranchers. Contact—possibly violent—between the Tasadays and civilization was inevitable. Fortunately, the anthropologists arrived first. Fortunate for *both* the Tasadays—and us!

The Philippine officials hope to protect the Tasadays by the establishment of large forest reserves in the mountains. Here the Tasadays will be allowed to remain unchanged if they choose.

By good management of the new agricultural and lumbering activities in the land around these mountain reserves, the government hopes to protect the environment. These border areas of controlled development may also provide opportunities to train and educate the Tasadays for their changing rôle in the modern world.

At the same time, the Tasadays may have much to teach modern man. Already research teams are with the Tasadays in the forest attempting to answer many questions about their lives. How can they survive without farming, metals, or permanent homes? What foods do they find free and wild in the forests? How much food is necessary for them to survive as a tribe? And how long can one area supply the group before it must move to another?

The Tasadays provide a rare opportunity for 20th century man to observe first-hand how his primitive ancestors lived. As true hunters and food-gatherers who still live off the land, the Tasadays offer a living demonstration of how man once existed in perfect harmony with his environment—indeed, as an integral part of the total ecological system.

FOUR MILLION AND TWENTY BLACKBIRDS

Four and twenty blackbirds baked into a pie may be a tasty dish to set before a king; but *four million and twenty* blackbirds in your back yard are a nightmare.

Many Americans thought it a joke when nearly four million cowbirds, grackles, and starlings descended on tiny Scotland Neck, North Carolina, in the early spring of 1969.

For the people of Scotland Neck, however, the blackbirds were no joke.

First, the birds made a horrible racket as they left their roosts in the morning and when they returned at night. Second, the droppings of four million birds have a vile and stomach-turning odor. Third, the lice and other parasites carried by the birds posed a serious health hazard.

When the birds didn't go away and when the droppings started to reach ankle depth and dead birds began to litter lawns, the people of Scotland Neck became frantic.

They even considered using some of the odd-ball suggestions for getting rid of the birds that came in from around the country. Like building giant scarecrows! Or shining bright searchlights on the birds so they couldn't sleep at night! Or playing loud rock music to drive the birds crazy!

One ingenious plan called for spraying the birds with detergent powder just before a rainstorm. Supposedly when the soap and rain washed away the protective body oils, the birds would freeze to death. The weather remained warm and clear in Scotland Neck, so the plan was never put in action. Perhaps it is just as well. No one ever considered what they would do with four million frozen blackbirds.

In desperation, scores of hunters went out and blasted away at the birds with shotguns. Only a relatively few birds were killed, however, and the rest simply flew back to the roosts when the hunters were finished firing.

Finally the birds just packed up and flew away. Apparently their stay in Scotland Neck was over and they were headed North to summer roosts.

But would they come back some other spring? Not likely, said the experts.

According to blackbird specialists, the half-billion American blackbirds usually migrate in great flocks of between 50,000 and one million birds. Although a flock may come back to the same general area each year, they rarely return to the exact same spot.

Well, anyhow, that's how the blackbirds are *supposed* to behave. Unfortunately the blackbirds who roosted in Scotland Neck didn't listen to the experts. Besides they seemed to like the place. And back they have come—year after year.

The return of the blackbirds has made Scotland Neck a minor tourist attraction. However, the townspeople would rather have peace and quiet.

Considering that every other anti-bird scheme has failed, the people of Scotland Neck now think they may have to cut down their trees so the birds will have no place to land.

THE PLANT OF MYSTERIOUS DEATH

In hundreds of old horror movies about haunted mansions in the Deep South, ghostly images of Spanish moss draped like death shrouds from decaying balconies and tree branches have provided a backdrop to terror.

Now, the Spanish moss—so often associated with mysterious death—is mysteriously dying itself.

Really neither "Spanish" nor a "moss," the plant is a very distant cousin of the pineapple with long stringy gray-green leaves and tiny yellowish blossoms. Found throughout the South from the Gulf Coast to Virginia, as well as in Central America and on the islands of the Caribbean, Spanish moss has often been falsely accused of being a killer itself. In fact, some people call it the "Vampire of the Forests."

The poor plant gained this rotten reputation because it is usually found festooning dead trees and people wrongly assumed that it sucked the life from other living plants. Actually, the plant is no killer. It takes nourishment from moisture and particles carried on the wind and simply clings to any structure—including light fixtures and telephone poles—that will provide a convenient anchor.

Ironically, *something in the air* now threatens to destroy this familiar symbol of the Old South. An unknown disease is killing off the moss everywhere.

Should the Spanish moss ever disappear, the South would lose the source of some very colorful legends. For example, the Indians claim the plant grew from the hair of a maiden who killed herself for the love of a young brave. Her long tresses have been draped over trees ever since, say the Indians, as a tribute to her lost lover.

The French explorers in Louisiana called the plant "Spanish beard" as an insult to their competing explorers in the New World. The Spanish returned the insult by dubbing the plant "French hair."

72

The early settlers—who finally stuck with the name Spanish moss—mixed the stringy plant with mud to make mortar for their cabins. They also used cured and dried moss to make bridles, horse collars, and saddle blankets. In the early part of this century, enterprising Southerners harvested the plant with knives tied to the end of long poles. They sold the fast-growing plant as stuffing for mattresses and padded furniture before the invention of synthetic padding materials.

Some day soon, perhaps, the Spanish moss could become just a legend itself. Unless, of course, science can find the cause—and the cure—for its mysterious malady.

The plant is usually resistant to all sorts of bugs, so scientists think the cause might be some new type of exotic plant virus. Other experts, however, think the answer may be more simple.

Because Spanish moss literally "lives on the air," one likely culprit for its killer is modern air pollution. If man doesn't clean up his air soon, the mysterious and ghostly Spanish moss may truly become a ghost.

THE SLOW EARTHQUAKE

For centuries the people of Naples, Italy, and surrounding towns have lived in the shadow of death. The sleeping Mt. Vesuvius across the bay is a constant reminder of the potential turmoil just beneath the earth's crust.

As if that wasn't enough, a part of the Pozzuoli slum section is known as the Campi Flegrei, or "fiery fields," and smoke and steam continually seep from ugly cracks in the soil.

For more than a decade, Pozzuoli also has been slowly rising out of the ground. In the spring of 1970, the rising suddenly accelerated and the streets and buildings lifted as much as three feet in some places.

Known to scientists as the "Pozzuoli Uplift," this strange phenomenon might be better described as a "slow earthquake."

Slow or not, the uplift caused serious destruction. Old rickety buildings suffered the most, as the shifting of foundations crumbled mortar and cracked stonework.

The worst problem, however, was the wave of panic and terror that swept through the grimy neighborhoods of the slum.

Daily reports from Pozzuoli claimed that new volcanic cracks had appeared in the fiery fields and that lava was oozing out. Jittery citizens reported earth tremors almost hourly.

Fishermen returned to the Bay of Naples with wild stories of finding cooked fish in blackened nets burned by undersea eruptions.

None of the stories—earthquakes, cracks, or cooked fish—could be verified by government officials. But this didn't stop people from panicking. Thousands fled their homes and angry editorials demanded government aid.

Pozzuoli had disaster on its mind and nothing could reduce the fear of being trapped in the packed tenements and narrow streets if the buildings collapsed.

The fear of Pozzuoli's people was not entirely foolish or irrational. Living in Pozzuoli is much like living on the lid of a boiling pot. As the heat under the pot increases and decreases, the water boils, bubbles and cools so that the lid rises and falls with the heat.

Some day—perhaps next century, or next year, or even tomorrow—the internal heat of the earth's burner may suddenly turn up to the point where the pot boils over and the Pozzuoli lid blows sky high.

INVASION OF THE BALLOON SPIDERS

"Unusual flying/floating material observed near St. Louis at McDonnell-Douglas Space Center. Bubble-shaped, filmy material drifting northward. Objects ranging from dime-size to 10-foot globules sighted."

When you operate a Center for Short-Lived Phenomena, you often receive all sorts of far-out reports about all sorts of far-out things. But this one was really far-out! In fact, it sounded like the typical "creatures-from-outer-space story."

"Samples retrieved appear to be fibrous material, pure white and sticky when in contact with grass, metal, or other objects. No cell structure visible even under an 800-power microscope."

What in the world could this be? Some horrible new kind of air pollution? The messy fall-out from some industrial smokestack?

Or, was it something from out of this world? The debris of an interstellar spacecraft that had exploded over our planet? Sticky gelatin bombs dropped by extraterrestrial invaders?

Actually, the strange white bubbles turned out to be made neither by men on this planet nor supermen on another. The weird floating fibers were the products of one of nature's oddest forms of reproduction.

The city of St. Louis had been invaded not by Martians, but by balloon spiders.

The answer to the puzzle came from biologists at the county health department. They found the material looked much like the thin strands of fiber spun by silkworms. More important, in one globule, they found a small brownish-yellow spider about the size of a penny.

The balloon spider is peculiar among the insects for its strange mating habits. The female climbs to the top of a tall tree where she spins a filmy circular web. Into this web, she deposits her eggs. Then she cuts the web loose so the wind can carry it off. Wherever the breeze carries the balloonlike web and its load of eggs, a new colony of spiders will spring up.

Farmers in Missouri are quite familiar with the drifting webs. But city dwellers seldom see the phenomenon. On the day of the St. Louis invasion, however, the wind and weather conditions were perfect for carrying the webs out of the country and into the downtown streets.

At the height of the "invasion," webs filled the air with a density of almost one per square foot. For city folk unaccustomed to nature's odd-ball ways, it was unbelievable. No wonder they thought the spider invasion was something from out of this world.

THE GREAT GASSER

In the fall of 1969, the Yugoslavian company Naftgas was boring a deep well near the little town of Becej on the Hungarian border. These modern prospectors were seeking natural gas, the prime source of heating and cooking fuel for many parts of Europe.

To their dismay, the Naftgas prospectors found much more gas than they could handle.

Suddenly and without warning, the drillers broke through an underground crystal block. The drill spun wildly for a few seconds, then a tremendous explosion lifted the drilling rig off the ground and a geyser of air shot out of the hole.

The drillers had inadvertently tapped a small gas volcano.

The man-made blow-hole emitted high pressure air for almost

six months. The worst part of the geyser was the horrible whistling noise caused by the escaping air. It sounded like a million screaming banshees.

The villagers of Becej had finally become accustomed to the terrible sound, when it suddenly stopped. For one day—April 9, 1970—an unnatural silence fell over Becej.

Officials from Naftgas gingerly inspected their creation. Could they start drilling again? Had the volcano stopped? Hardly!

Again without warning, the well suddenly exploded. This time the eruption sent great clods of earth hurtling hundreds of yards into the air. A large dirty cloud rose over the well. When the smoke and dust cleared, the drillers and villagers found a huge crater more than 100 feet wide. And out of this crater seeped the noxious deadly natural gas—93 per cent carbon dioxide and seven per cent methane.

That night, five people in Becej died from gas poisoning, another ten were hospitalized. The government ordered the town evacuated and the well capped, if possible.

Workers poured thousands of gallons of water into the well to break down the gas. Huge motor driven fans were set up to purify the air. Still, the crater continued to rumble and grumble for almost two months. Occasionally large hunks of earth shot into the air like mortar shells.

Then, on June 4, the eruptions stopped once more. This time, however, the calm lasted only 30 minutes. An ear-splitting explosion rocked the town and a piece of earth as large as a small building shot from the crater's mouth.

But this was the geyser's last gasp. The walls of the 400-foot-deep crater fell in on themselves, sealing off the gas flow forever.

Today, there are few drilling operations around Becej. No one wants to create another man-made volcano.

A BLACK CHRISTMAS

On Christmas morning 1969, children living around Lake Vattern in southern Sweden looked out the windows and began to cry. As far as the eye could see, the white mantle of Christmas snow had turned jet black.

Fresh snow had fallen on Lake Vattern for several days before Christmas. Then, on Christmas Eve, the snow had turned to a light, freezing rain.

Now, on this Christmas morning, the bright, gay, winter landscape had turned dark and dull. Every inch of the ground was black and grimy, just as if evil elves had painted it, playing a cruel joke.

Deer and rabbits running through the fields seemed as puzzled as the children. When the animals ran over the snow, their hoofs and paws turned up white tracks. Apparently, the black snow was only on the surface and had probably fallen with the rain.

Whatever it was, the black material was certainly gritty, and almost impossible to remove from clothing, even with strong detergents. Tracked inside, the black snow melted into little shiny pools of oily liquid.

One of the most famous writers about the mysterious ways of nature, Charles Fort, once compiled an entire book devoted to unexplained and mysterious "rains and snows." Fort claimed to have seen falls of red snow, fish, flowers, and even frogs. Unfortunately, few of Fort's amazing incidents were ever studied or documented by reliable eyewitnesses or scientists.

Today, Fort's stories remain only oddities, more fiction than fact. But there is no fiction about Sweden's black snow of 1969.

A team of scientists from Stockholm's Ecological Center rushed to Lake Vattern immediately for a first-hand investigation. They analyzed the black snow—and found it contained dangerously high levels of DDT as well as a host of other industrial pollutants.

Unlike that mysterious "rain of frogs" reported by Charles Fort, there was no question about this snowfall. It was the work of man.

Sweden's black snow was still another example of how industrial pollution is ruining the atmosphere and destroying the beauty of our planet. Indeed, for the children of Lake Vattern, pollution even stole Christmas.

SQUIRRELS ON THE MARCH

Motorists travelling the highways of the East Coast in September 1968 were the first to notice something strange was happening to the grey squirrels.

Almost 1,000 times as many dead squirrels as usual littered the roads. The sight of dead animals on our high-speed expressways is common, but when unusual numbers of bodies appear on the asphalt, biologists know something odd is happening in the bushes too.

Farmers, hunters, and game wardens confirmed these suspicions. Throughout the Appalachian region of Maryland, Virginia, Tennessee, and the Carolinas, thousands of grey squirrels were seen scurrying through the underbrush, moving across open areas, invading suburban gardens, and even swimming in reservoirs and rivers.

Typically, the nation's newspapers overreacted to the story and distorted the facts. According to press reports, "gigantic hordes of hungry squirrels were headed north in a mass migration caused by disease, starvation, and insanity."

Many well-meaning and soft-hearted Americans were so moved by the plight of the "hungry and tired" squirrels that they launched campaigns to feed them. Supermarket posters in North Carolina urged people to establish feeding stations. People sent checks to the state Fish and Game Departments to pay for squirrel food. And one group of Tennessee citizens even appealed to the people of Florida to gather acorns for shipment North.

Less kind-hearted, but more practical, hunters urged state game wardens to open the squirrel season early and double the bag limits.

Professional biologists found the public reaction funny, but they were no less fascinated by the strange squirrel behavior. The behavior was even more mysterious when all the popular theories about its cause proved false.

For example, almost all the squirrels had bellies full of black cherries and acorn mash, so they certainly weren't hungry. Nor did they seem bothered by sickness or even parasites that could have driven them nutty.

In fact, the scientists couldn't even find any indication that the squirrels were travelling in flocks or headed northward. Most of the squirrels seemed determined individualists, travelling alone —and headed in every direction imaginable.

The biologists did find, however, that the squirrel population was unusually large that fall. The strange behavior was related to this overpopulation—but not because they had been driven crazy by overcrowding.

Similar squirrel "migrations" had been recorded before. In the days of the last century, before the great forests had been cut down, they were quite common.

Strangely enough, all the migrations also took place in September. Why did the squirrels start moving about so wildly at harvest time when the food was the most plentiful?

The answer to this puzzle is found in the peculiar habits of the grey squirrel, the type of squirrel found in most big city parks.

Unlike his cousin the red squirrel, the grey squirrel doesn't store his food in a hollow tree. He simply tucks nuts and seeds under leaves or a few inches of dirt. This storage technique naturally uses up a lot more territory than if he simply picked one central spot.

Each fall, the grey squirrels go through a major "reshuffle." As they run about looking for acorns and new and different spots to stash them away, the squirrels move farther and farther away from their regular haunts. Sometimes they even invade back yards or swim across rivers in search of new hunting and hiding grounds.

Away from their regular haunts, the squirrels easily become confused and disoriented when frightened. In short, they act crazy.

The so-called "migrating squirrels" were really doing what comes naturally. However, there were so many more of them in the fall of 1968, they caught the attention of people usually not interested in squirrel behavior.

Biologists warn that more of these "migrations" may be on the way. The growing concern for ecology and conservation is helping to preserve and create more forest land, and, in turn, more squirrels. Those furry travellers with the bushy tails may be a common sight in the Septembers of the future.

CATCH A FALLING STAR

Gunther (Skip) Schwartz is one of those rare humans who know how it feels to catch a falling star.

On Saturday night, January 3, 1970, Skip sat watching television in his home in Lincoln, Nebraska. Suddenly, the news announcer interrupted with the report that an incredibly bright fireball had just streaked over the Midwest, spewing sparks and smoke behind it.

Most other men would simply have switched off the television and gone to bed. But Skip Schwartz bolted from his chair and began calling television stations and airports for more information.

The reason for Skip's unusual reaction to this news is his unusual job. Skip is the field manager of the Smithsonian's Prairie Network, a system of 16 automatic camera stations spread over seven states to photograph fireballs (super-economy-size falling stars) and to help recover meteorites (the extraterrestrial material that creates the fireball's light and sometimes falls on earth as space debris).

The eyewitness report of an astronomer in Kansas indicated that any meteorite from this fireball might have fallen somewhere in either southeastern Kansas or northeastern Oklahoma.

Skip immediately called the camera station caretakers in these areas and asked that films be sent to network headquarters in Lincoln. When the films arrived and were developed two days later, they showed a brilliant fireball trail, brighter than the full moon and lasting some 9 seconds. Using a computer to compare photos from two different stations, scientists plotted the fireball's path to the ground and predicted the possible impact point to be near the tiny hamlet of Lost City, Oklahoma.

Skip bundled himself and a pile of maps into a truck and headed south to Oklahoma. He hoped this wouldn't be another

wild goose chase. Most fireballs burn up completely. Even if a meteorite does fall on the ground, it is like looking for the proverbial needle in a haystack. After five years of photographing the sky and searching the ground, the Smithsonian had not yet recovered a single meteorite.

But this time would be different!

At the start, the situation looked as bad as usual. A nine-inch snowfall covered the ground just before Skip Schwartz arrived in Lost City. It was two days before the weather cleared and he could venture out on the lonely roads.

On one such snow-covered road, only a half-mile from the predicted impact point, Skip drove over a black rock about the size and shape of a Vienna breadloaf. Something about this rock made him stop and pick it up. Just one look and he became hysterical with joy.

He had accidentally driven right into the object of his search.

This heavy, dark-crusted, smooth-surfaced stone was the Lost City Meteorite!

Of all the hundreds of meteorites found by scores of men in tens of centuries, the Lost City Meteorite is one of the most valuable. Not only did the quick recovery time (less than a week from fall to lab!) make possible delicate measurements of radio-activities created in space, but the photographic record of its fall even told scientists what part of space it came from.

More important for Skip Schwartz—he had finally caught his falling star.

THE GREAT FROG WAR

For six days the battle raged through the jungle in Southeast Asia. More than 10,000 warriors tore into each other, killing and wounding hundreds in a battle that swung back and forth.

A clash between the allies and communists in Vietnam? A guerrilla raid on some government outpost? A tribal battle?

Not really. The fierce warriors in this strange battle were 10 different species of frogs and toads apparently fighting to the death.

"The Great Frog War" began on November 8, 1970 as a small skirmish between about 50 frogs in a jungle clearing near the Malaysian seaport of Sungai Siup. The numbers quickly swelled, and, by the end of the day, some 3,000 frogs were biting and ripping at each other.

The next day the battle resumed in the shadow of an ancient Hindu temple. The swamp soon became a swirling mass of green, yellow, brown, and grey bodies, all clawing and tearing and making horrible sounds. Residents of the area who gathered to watch the strange fight claimed the frogs even carried off their dead and wounded.

Other smaller fights continued for almost a week. Eventually, an estimated 10,000 frogs and toads joined the battle. Local natives claimed the war was an annual event, with the frogs fighting over choice feeding and breeding grounds.

However, scientists from the Zoology Department at the University of Malaya had another explanation. In a report to the Smithsonian Center, the Malaysian biologists told of visiting the battle scene and finding the swamp waters full of frog eggs and tadpoles.

This had been no "war," they said, but rather an amphibian sex orgy!

The frogs simply were doing what came naturally—mating during a rainy spell that had followed a long drought. Unfortunately, the noise and activity of the mating attracted a species of toad that secretes a poisonous substance from its skin fatal to frogs.

Sometimes, too, as the big bullfrogs fought for the attentions of females, they jumped at each other, biting and tearing with their claws. Some frogs also had abrasive skin on their chests that ripped the hides of the others.

Despite all the appearances of a deadly battle, the frogs really were *making love, not war.*

The so-called "Frog War" had an odd sidelight. The superstitious people of Malaysia think the frog wars are bad omens of terrible disasters to come. In 1969, just 12 days before the bloody Malay-Chinese race riots that killed thousands of people, frogs had battled in a swamp near Butterworth, Malaysia. In years past, other wars supposedly had preceded floods, storms, and major revolutions.

"Pure nonsense," said most scientists, discounting any relationship between the frog wars and other calamities.

Yet, just one day after the "Great Frog War of 1970" ended, a gigantic cyclone roared up the Bay of Bengal and struck nearby East Pakistan killing a half-million people.

Only a coincidence? Who knows?

A BROWN WAVE OF ANTS

Jose Castellanos worked a tiny farm in the Lares Valley of Peru. This lush, green land is well-known for its tea- and cocoa-leaf production. It is a rich and beautiful valley.

Jose was proud of his small plot of land and its bountiful crop of cocoa plants. At harvest time, he happily cut his own crop and carried it to market. His farm provided well for his small family.

One morning in early 1969, Jose awoke to hear a strange, rustling noise, almost as if a brush fire was burning downwind in the valley. Jose jumped from his straw pallet and rushed outside. He saw no smoke, but the weird noise seemed to be coming closer.

He climbed a small knoll behind his hut and peered into the early morning mist toward the sound. Jose choked with fear, for what he saw was worse than any fire.

91

Slowly moving down the valley toward his cocoa plants was a great, coffee-colored wave. Millions upon millions of giant brown ants were sweeping down the valley like some mammoth lawn mower.

Behind the ants, the green vegetation of the valley—the precious tea and cocoa plants, the fruits and vegetables, even the green grass of lawns—had disappeared. In their wake, the ants left a beige and barren wasteland.

The ants that destroyed the Lares and La Convencion valleys of southern Peru in 1969 were known as the *Coqui*, a species of destructive leaf-cutting ants.

This type of ant has been a traditional scourge of farmers in the tropics, but rarely did they attack in such numbers as this year. Every farmer in Peru's valleys prepares for these insects, but none were ready to face the millions this time. The sheer number of ants in this "invasion" made control virtually impossible.

Worse yet, these ants had a special fondness for the tea and cocoa leaves that were the pride of the Lares Valley. An entire tea or cocoa plant could be denuded within seconds by the hungry insects.

Eventually, after destroying thousands of dollars worth of crops, the ants turned away from the cultivated land and headed for the open fields. Eventually, too, simple overpopulation killed the ants, for the countryside simply could not support their enormous numbers.

Although many farmers were ruined by the invasion of the ants, the situation could have been much worse.

In some parts of South America, there are species of ants that eat animal flesh as well as plants. Hordes of army ants have reportedly eaten entire forests, including any animals—and humans—unfortunate enough to be caught in their path.

A PUSHMI-PULLYU EARTH

Sometimes strange changes in the earth's surface happening halfway around the world from each other seem oddly linked together.

For example, while the natives of Ticrapo, Peru, watched their little city slowly sink into the earth, people half a world away on the Philippine island of Davao Oriental watched a huge bubble of dirt bulge out of the ground.

Messengers from Ticrapo brought an incredible tale to government officials in the capital. Their homes and farms were dropping into the bowels of the earth! Indeed, a circle of land about 1 mile wide had cracked, split, and fallen several inches lower than the surrounding countryside.

The simple adobe farm houses of the town leaned at crazy angles like stubby Towers of Pisa. Buildings appeared ready to collapse at any second and the farmers moved their families and possessions to safer ground.

Almost within days of the Ticrapo sinking, the Smithsonian Institution received word of an equally odd happening near Baganda on the island of Davao Oriental in the Philippines. A huge earthmound had pushed up out of the ground near the northern bank of the Mahanob River.

The bulging nob of land, some 150 feet long and 15 feet high, was located at the base of a long gentle ridge leading to the island's main mountain range. Large cracks appeared along the ridge and a small stream that once flowed beneath it had risen out of the ground so its dry bed traced a path up the side of the hill.

The dramatic rising of the earth had happened quickly, popping up some dozen feet in less than three weeks. At the same time, earthquake tremors shook the region and the sound of crushing or sliding rocks could be heard.

What was the connection between the land rise at Baganda and the land sink at Ticrapo thousands of miles away? None at all, said most scientists. Although they agreed the earth is really a plastic body constantly changing shape, this case of a simultaneous push and pull on the planet's surface was only a coincidence.

The land rise in the Philippines was a phenomenon known as "slumping," that is, the underground movement of dirt and boulders due to erosion. If the subsurface landslide is suddenly stopped, the dirt creates a weird pile-up that looks like a bulge in the ground.

The Ticrapo sinking, on the other hand, probably was due to a weak earthquake in which the land simply shifted and settled along a major crack in the earth's crust.

Coincidence or not, the rise and fall of the earth on opposite sides of the world almost looked as if some playful giant had poked his finger into the ground at Ticrapo and watched it poke out at Baganda on the other side of the planet.

THE BLOODY TIDE

All along the Louisiana coast in June 1969, fishermen, off-shore oil riggers, and beachcombers watched in amazement as the water turned red almost before their eyes.

As the tide rolled into the bayous of Terrebonne, La Fourche, Jefferson, and Plaquemines parishes, the water swirled scarlet around cypress trees and lapped pinkly against beaches.

Then, right behind this strange red tide, came wave after wave of dead fish.

According to estimates by the Louisiana Fish and Wildlife Commission, more than 125 tons of fish, including menhaden, trout, crab, shrimp, and sting rays washed up along a 120-mile stretch of coast west of the Mississippi Delta. All were apparently victims of the mysterious red tide.

Actually, the red tide was no mystery to biologists. "Red tide" is the popular name for a rare biological event that is brief, spectacular, and deadly to underwater inhabitants.

The water really turns red from the flowers of a tiny, almost microscopic, aquatic plant that usually blooms in the late summer or early fall. As it blooms, the plant not only colors the water, it releases a poisonous substance deadly to fish.

Ironically, the organism is itself extremely fragile and deteriorates shortly after it blooms. But not before it has done its deadly job.

Massive killings of fish from other red tides have been reported occasionally along the Gulf of Mexico coast. (A similar red tide off the shores of Peru in December 1970 killed literally millions of fish!)

The Louisiana red tide came early and unexpectedly. Apparently weather conditions, water temperature, and even mineral content of the sea were perfect for promoting the bloom. Other aquatic plants have similar life cycles and may also cause multicolored tides, but only a few produce the toxic substances capable of killing.

Unfortunately, there is no way to predict—or prevent—the more deadly forms of the tide. The men who watch the waters along the Gulf Coast only know that when the water runs blood-red, death usually follows in its wake.

THE BURNING SOIL

Farmers walking to their gardens in western Samar one morning in 1969 noticed that the ground beneath their feet seemed unusually warm.

The weather in this part of the Philippine Islands had been extremely dry and hot for several weeks. Still, the ground couldn't get that hot from the sun!

Then, as the farmers stared in disbelief, thin wisps of smoke drifted up between their toes.

The ground was on fire!

The Philippines lie on one of the great "rings of fire" that encircle the Pacific. Volcanic activity in this area of the world is very common and horribly violent. The terrified natives of Samar thought the burning soil certainly must be a warning of some terrible eruption about to occur.

Yet, for many days afterward, the fields of Samar continued to smolder without any volcanic eruption. The lush, green covering of grass and reeds turned brown, then black, and then finally died. Gigantic coconut trees, their roots burned through, tumbled to the ground with a crash, sending up little clouds of ashes and burnt twigs.

But still no eruption. The land simply smoked. The ground became covered with a thin layer of ashes. And a veil of white smoke hung over the island farmlands.

Finally a team of scientists from the Commission on Volcanology arrived from Manila for an inspection tour. They found no evidence of volcanic activity, but their discovery was even more unbelievable.

They found the soil at Samar as inflammable as a Molotov cocktail!

The Samar dirt is black, lumpy, porous, and filled with hydrocarbons. In other words, the soil is really a mixture of dirt and vegetable matter much like the ancient swamps. In many parts of the world, this rich earth was pushed deep beneath the surface eons ago to become underground deposits of coal and oil.

At Samar, this mixture lies close to the surface. It is just like old oily rags—ready to burst into flames under the right conditions. The long dry spell in Samar had made the ground highly combustible, so that a campfire or a carelessly discarded match could touch off an underground blaze.

Apparently the "Samar soil burn" had started in some cultivated land and then spread slowly and undetected beneath the surface until it engulfed more than sixty acres of land. Over 35,000 coconut and other fruit trees were destroyed before the underground fire burned itself out.

THE SEA SURGE AT VALPARAISO

Sometimes physical changes in the earth occur so far away from human settlements that they go unnoticed and unrecorded. Yet, all events in nature are interrelated and every action has a counter reaction.

On July 25, 1968, unusually high waves began rolling into shore along the coast of Chile. Waves more than 18 feet high swelled into harbors. At Valparaiso, ships bobbed wildly, broke their moorings, and crashed into docks.

Thousands of little fishing boats tossed and bucked in the churning surf, frightening their superstitious crews who had seen no signs of an approaching storm. The waves struck suddenly and without warning and then ceased as quickly as they had begun.

High waves along the coast of Chile are often caused by northerly winds, but there had been no breezes that day. Nor could scientists record any off-shore earthquake activity that might have triggered these near-tidal waves.

What was the source of these mysterious and murderous waves? Why had the sea surged forth at Valparaiso?

Most experts agree the waves could only have been created by some great underwater disturbance somewhere far out in the Pacific. Perhaps thousands of miles away, on a barren and deserted atoll, a volcano had erupted in terrible fury. Or maybe an earthquake caused by the spreading of the sea bed along one of the great cracks in the ocean floor had churned up the waves that would some later day strike Chile.

Earthquakes in the Philippines and volcanoes in the Fiji Islands had caused similar tidal waves in the past. Unfortunately, this time, no report of unusual activity had been received from any part of the Pacific.

The exact cause of the sea surge at Valparaiso has never been determined. Somewhere, sometime, at some unknown spot in the vast Pacific, the waves had begun rolling eastward toward Chile. Days, weeks, maybe even months later, these waves crashed, unexpected and unpredicted, against the shore.

The waves were man's only evidence that something strange and powerful had torn apart the ocean's floor many, many miles away.

THE FATAL FLOWERS

When the woodlands of America burst into bloom each spring, this country rejoices in the beauty of nature. When the bamboo forests of Japan begin to flower, that country goes into mourning.

No, this Japanese despair over the blooming bamboo is not just a strange Oriental custom. Bamboo is a very valuable commodity in Japan; and once the unusual ma-dake species of bamboo flowers, it dies.

The ma-dake bamboo is a type of "century plant" that blooms only once every hundred years. (Actually, the cycle runs between 60 and 120 years, depending on the average temperature of the area where it grows.)

This fatal flowering usually affects entire forests at the same time. In other words, all the plants of the same "generation" that are born together, live, flower, and die together too.

The blooming of bamboo in a particular region usually lasts from one to fifteen years. But the end result is always the same. About a year after the flowers appear, the greenish-yellow stalks wither.

The latest cycle of blooming and dying began in 1960, when about 30 percent of the Japanese bamboo crop burst into blossoms and then wilted away. The peak of the current flowering came in 1969, when almost 50 percent of the remaining bamboo forests were affected.

Unlike other plants, the flowers of the bamboo produce no fruits or seeds. Instead, the bamboo reproduces itself by sending out new roots.

The roots are usually unaffected by cutting or breaking healthy bamboo. But the flowering death kills even the roots. Almost ten years is required for new roots to take hold and to produce new and harvestable crops after the blooming.

Obviously, in Japan, where bamboo is used for construction, paper-making, art, and thousands of other purposes, the once-a-century appearance of those deadly flowers is catastrophic.

Imagine how Americans would feel if the pine, evergreen, and redwood forests wilted and died every one hundred years.

THE FLOATING ISLAND

The Navy lookout on the destroyer escort *John D. Pearce* couldn't believe his eyes.

Out there, in the middle of the Windward Passage, halfway between Cuba and Haiti and 60 miles from any land, a tiny island was floating along at two and a half knots.

Floating islands have been part of sea lore since the Phoenicians first sailed out into the Atlantic. Some of the legends have a basis in truth, for large chunks of coastline do often break loose and drift out to sea. The matted undergrowth and roots help hold the soil together and keep it afloat.

The 15-yard-long island spotted by the escort ship was covered with a bushy mangrovelike growth. It also sprouted about a dozen 35-foot palm trees.

Of course, the island had to be reported immediately as a

hazard to navigation. But naval authorites were not the only people excited by this odd discovery.

Ecologists at the Smithsonian Institution who heard about the island thought it would make a fine floating laboratory to test some theories about ecology. For example, how do land animals and plants fare at sea? Would new ecological chains develop in this floating environment? Most important, if the island docked at some other body of land, would the plants and animals take up new homes on the mainland?

Perhaps this mysterious island might hold the key to explaining how various species of plants and animals had been scattered around the world.

Seeking answers to these and other questions, a team of scientists rushed from Washington to the U.S. Naval Base at Guantanamo Bay, Cuba, to catch a special island-hunting helicopter.

After catching up with the floating island, the scientists hoped to lower themselves by rope ladder to make on-the-spot investigations and gather samples of the flora and fauna. Later, they'd keep track of the island's drifting, mark its possible landfall, and monitor any cross-cultivation between the island and its new home.

Unfortunately, floating islands prefer to remain mysteries—a part of the ocean mythology with mermaids and sea monsters.

Even before the scientists boarded their helicopter, the island sank unseen and unmarked somewhere south of Cuba. Any secrets it might have revealed went with it to the bottom of the Caribbean.

THE CORAL KILLERS

A massive, unexplained, and almost unstoppable population explosion among a once rare species of starfish is threatening to destroy the entire ecological balance of the South Pacific.

For more than a decade, marine biologists have watched with horror as the ugly, sixteen-legged, Crown of Thorns starfish has multiplied out of control.

No one would really care about the Crown of Thorns—if only it wasn't so hungry! The starfish's favorite meal is coral, and the creature—which grows up to two feet wide—can devour an area of coral twice its own size in less than twenty four hours.

Coral is really a tiny animal that secretes a calcium solution. As the calcium oozes out of the coral and hardens into a shell, the coral builds underwater caves that harbor millions of fish and create tough natural breakwaters that protect island beaches.

Once a coral reef is attacked and eaten by the starfish, it begins to crumble and wash away. With the coral reef gone, the fish lose their homes and the beaches become vulnerable to the battering of ocean waves. Eventually, the food supply for millions of people could disappear. Indeed, the very islands of the Pacific could disappear too.

"If the starfish population explosion continues unchecked," warn marine biologists, "the result could be a disaster unparalleled in the history of mankind."

The starfish first appeared in large numbers in 1963 at Green Island, a resort area on the edge of Australia's Great Barrier Reef. By 1969, the Crown of Thorns population had reached incredible proportions. And Australian scientists claimed the starfish were "eating their way from one end of the Reef to the other."

Destruction was not restricted to Australia, however. The starfish invaded the waters around Guam, Truk, Rota, Johnston, the Fijis, and hundreds of other islands throughout the Pacific and Indian Oceans. At Guam, the Crown of Thorns population jumped from a handful to more than 20,000 in just three years and they ate up nearly 24 miles of coral.

After destroying one reef, the hungry starfish migrate to another. Often the smaller starfish remain behind to feed on any coral that has survived and started to grow again.

By mid-1969, the governments of all the nations touching the Pacific had begun action to halt the deadly starfish. But, although science was ready to fight the plague, no one really knew how it began. Whatever the cause, it probably involved some action by man.

The uncontrolled use of pesticides may have killed off some natural enemy of the starfish. Or, perhaps the widespread gathering of the giant Triton shell—the greatest enemy of the starfish—by natives for sale to collectors and tourists may have reduced the number of shells to the point where the starfish could multiply unchecked. Some scientists even think that underwater blasting or atomic tests could have touched off the sudden growth of the Crown of Thorns. Ironically, coral itself is a natural enemy of the starfish, feeding on its larva stage. If enough coral was destroyed by underwater explosions, the baby starfish might have started growing faster than the coral could eat them.

The job of halting the starfish explosion may prove as difficult as finding its cause. The surest method sends down individual divers to kill the starfish with injections of poison. Another method might be to release some new natural enemy of the starfish in the reefs. An important part of any attack will be an education program for the natives to halt the collecting of the giant Triton shells, still the best protection against the Crown of Thorns.

The battle to save the coral reefs will be long and costly. Yet, if it isn't fought—and won!—the Crown of Thorns could turn the Pacific into a vast dead sea.

THE MONSTER THAT WASN'T

The story out of Mexico sounded like a rerun of the *Creature from the Black Lagoon.*

According to United Press International, a 35-ton, 30-foot, unidentified sea creature had washed up on the beach at Tecolutla.

The creature's serpentlike body was covered with armor plate and jointed so it could swim. Most amazing, the so-called monster had a ten-foot horn protruding from its head.

The breathless report speculated that the creature might be a survivor from the age of dinosaurs somehow preserved in an iceberg for millions of years. Or, the story suggested, the creature might have been driven from a dark, deep submarine cave by recent underwater blasting in the area.

This scanty report was both unbelievable and intriguing. In the early 1950's, African fishermen netted a specimen of fish thought extinct since prehistoric times. Could the Mexican sea monster be another of these lost animals?

Skeptical, but hopeful, officials at the Smithsonian Institution sent off urgent telegrams asking for more information.

Within hours, a telegram came back from a Mexican biologist who claimed to have investigated the carcass personally. He confirmed the general size and shape of the creature and reported:

"The animal has some kind of horn approximately 30 inches long and about three inches in diameter. It is not straight, but has a very small curvature—definitely the shape of a horn, not a bone.

"I feel the creature is a kind of mammal and certainly not a fish."

The so-called biologist may have been convinced the creature was not a fish, but the Smithsonian still thought the story sounded a bit fishy. Especially since no one had ever heard of the "biologist" before.

While marine biologists around the world waited for news, the Smithsonian asked the Biological Science Institute at Tampico, Mexico, to check out the monster.

Finally, several days later, the Smithsonian received a cable from a team of well-known scientists at the Institute.

The monster was nothing more than a common whale!

Apparently, the ill-fated creature had been attacked by sharks and its partly eaten body washed up on the shore. The horn was not a horn at all, but only a part of the skull that had fractured and split from the main bone.

The sea monster story had been all an elaborate hoax. Superstitious natives—and an imaginative reporter—had turned the grotesque decomposing body into a mysterious monster.

The so-called "biologist," who first confirmed that the creature and its horn were real, was never heard from again.

109

For a few days, however, marine biologists had held their breath—hoping for something truly unexpected and unbelievable. Perhaps some day a real creature from the past will be discovered. It is unlikely, of course, but science-fiction fans and scientists, too, still keep hoping.

INVASION OF THE GIANT SNAILS

The people of Miami, Florida, thought they had become victims of some horrible science-fiction nightmare when their pleasant, sunny residential neighborhoods were invaded by giant snails—some as big as a man's hand.

Perhaps "invasion" is not the right word. The snails actually were *brought* to Miami by some unsuspecting tourist who spotted the unusual shelled creatures in the tropics and thought they might make nice souvenirs.

Unfortunately, the giant snails—known as African snails or *Achatina fulica*—have plenty of natural enemies in other parts of the world, but few in Florida. Unchecked by normal forces, the snails began reproducing at a fantastic rate.

Because their appetites match their size, the giant snails created a giant problem for the Florida Department of Agriculture. The officials had visions of the snails gobbling up every bit of green vegetation in this famous resort.

Soon after the discovery of this potential snail plague, the state officials launched a massive extermination campaign. Just one week after posion bait was dropped in a 40-acre area, 2,500 dead snails were picked up. Two weeks later another 5,000 were found. By the end of the year, some 17,000 giant snails had been killed.

The Department of Agriculture didn't stop its extermination campaign even after this killing. Actually, they couldn't afford to stop!

The giant snails often go into a form of hibernation, remaining hidden and alive in some cool spot for more than 6 months. At the same time, the life-span of these big snails is about five years. And the typical snail mother drops some 400 to 600 eggs a year. Under perfect conditions, then, even one surviving snail could be responsible for producing 11 *billion off-spring* in five years.

Why, those snails could have eaten up all of Florida, Georgia, Alabama, and South Carolina and still be hungry!

Luckily, the snails now seem to be stopped. By late 1970, Florida officials reported finding only 5 to 10 snails a week. But the snail watch goes on, just in case the population starts to explode again.

THE VOLCANO THAT FELL IN

Time seems to have stopped two million years ago on the Galapagos Islands.

This weird world, 580 miles off the coast of Ecuador in the Pacific Ocean, is filled with plants and animals that exist nowhere else, including some throwbacks to prehistoric times.

More than 100 years ago, these bleak volcanic islands served as the living lab for testing Darwin's theory of evolution. Even today, modern biologists are thrilled by the sight of otter-sized iguanas (land lizards), four-eyed fish, scalesia trees (thirty-foot-high members of the dandelion family), and a host of other rare birds, plants, and insects.

In this topsy-turvey land of ancient relics, everything seems upside down. No wonder then, when the biggest volcano on the islands erupted, it fell *into the earth* instead of out of it.

On June 11, 1968, seismic monitoring stations around the world reported that a volcano on the uninhabited island of Fernandina had erupted with all the force of a multimegaton hydrogen bomb.

A huge mushroom cloud rose high above Fernandina. Many smaller explosions followed the first blast. During the night, volcanic dust in the atmosphere over the island sparked tremendous electrical storms, creating a scene straight out of Hell.

From all appearances, the island looked as if it had been destroyed completely. Scientists everywhere feared that lava flows might wipe out the precious living samples of rare plants and animals.

They were surprised and pleased, however, to find that the volcano had not blown its top like most others. Instead of spewing rocks and lava over the nearby countryside, the caldera (or crater floor) had simply collapsed, dropping almost 300 yards deeper into the bowels of the earth. The collapse caused incredible noise and dust—but little destruction outside the crater.

The first research team reached the rim of the Fernandina Caldera about a week later. The ground still shook with almost continuous tremors.

"The frequency and violence of these tremors was so great," reported one scientist, "that we counted 56 in less than six hours. Each lasted from two to six seconds and caused rock slides all around us.

"Trees shuddered as though a strong wind blew their branches. The tremors rose and fell in waves, so the whole island seemed balanced on top of a jellylike mass."

This continual shaking caused large sections of the crater rim—some more than 1,000 yards long—to fall into the depths. Avalanches of stones fell constantly to the floor of the crater that lay hidden under dust many yards below. The sound of falling rocks was like the roar of heavy seas. And strong gusts of wind rushed out of the crater after each avalanche.

A lake, once located in the northwestern part of the crater, had shifted almost a half-mile to the southeast. A large population of the rare Galapagos ducks had once lived in this little lake. No sign of them could now be found.

Aside from the ducks, however, there seemed few other casualties. Although every part of the island was covered with a light film of grey-black volcanic ash, most of the damage was inside the crater.

Luckily for science, the Fernandina volcano had been an *eruption in reverse*. The crater floor had collapsed from a lack of underground pressure, rather than exploding up and out from a build-up of gas and lava.

In the weird world of the Galapagos—where everything is backwards—this reverse eruption had helped save untold numbers of rare plants and animals that could never be replaced.

Perhaps nature sometimes tries to save its own creatures.

THE SLIDING GRAPES

Old Mrs. Udvari lived high on the steep bank of the Danube River near the Hungarian city of Dunafoldvar. With a few chickens and a pig, she lived a simple life of few luxuries. Her only joy was tending the tiny vineyard of fine purple grapes that climbed the slope outside her small, two-room, stone house.

One autumn afternoon, as Mrs. Udvari napped, a low rumbling sound and a fearsome shaking jolted her from sleep. She ran to the window of her trembling house just in time to see her precious vineyard slide down the hill toward the river.

Even before she could grasp what had happened, the floor of her home slipped from under her feet, the walls tumbled around her, and she and the shattered stones slid down the hillside after the grapes.

Several minutes later, bruised and battered, Mrs. Udvari pulled herself from the wreckage of her house and discovered that she had fallen more than 25 yards down the slope. And so had her beloved vineyard. Incredibly, the entire vineyard sat beside her—intact!

All the vine props still stood straight, each row arranged just as neat as before. Indeed, not even a single grape seemed out of place.

Mrs. Udvari and her vineyard had been caught in a very unusual landslide that occurred on September 15, 1971, at Dunafoldvar, just south of Budapest on the western bank of the Danube.

Other minor landslides had often occurred near here, for the river banks are high and steep and their soil is soft and rich.

The 1971 landslide was bigger than any in recent history and had all the earmarks of a major earthquake. More than a million cubic yards of earth slid into the river. A tremendous dust cloud rose over the area. And violent waves washed back and forth across the river.

116

When the dust settled and the waters calmed, people found that two new islands, both long and narrow, running parallel to the bank, had been created in the river.

Naturally, everyone assumed that the islands had been formed by debris sliding into the water from the high bank above. But later research proved this wrong. Instead, something very odd had happened at Dunafoldvar.

Both islands were approximately 900 feet long and some 30 feet wide. Their surfaces were split by great cracks and studded with crazily tilted blocks of clay bigger than a man. They looked like small mountain ranges poking up from the water.

More puzzling, however, was the discovery that the islands seemed composed of the same material as the river bed. In fact, shells, snails, and fish carcasses dotted their surfaces. Obviously, these new islands had not slid into the river from above, but had been pushed up from below!

Investigations showed that torrential rains had fallen for several weeks before the slide and probably loosened the earth beneath the surface. This substrata apparently started sliding downhill, at first leaving the top soil undisturbed. Because most of the movement was in the lower depths of the river bank, the ground beneath became compressed, thus forcing the river bed to push upward out of the water and create the islands.

For Mrs. Udvari, this strange landslide produced one happy side-effect. Although her stone house couldn't withstand the shock, her well-rooted vineyard held together. Anchored in a layer of top soil, the vineyard simply rode down the river bank on top of the landslide to its new location without any damage.

THE CAT AND MOUSE CAPER

Invasion! Invasion!

In 1972, two very different parts of the world faced invasions by two very different kinds of animals. Unusually large numbers of a wildcat known as the Canadian Lynx were seen slipping over the border into Minnesota and other northern states. And, half-way around the world, in Queensland, Australia, millions of mice overran farms, fields, and houses.

The reason for the invasions: population explosions.

For example, the Canadian lynx—a scrappy little wildcat noted for the long tufts of hair on its eartips—is normally rare south of the Canadian border. However, in the winter of 1972, scores of lynxes were spotted throughout Minnesota, North Dakota, and other adjacent states.

Wildlife experts suspect these wandering wildcats were pushed south by overcrowding in the Canadian north woods. With their normal hunting grounds stripped clean by a population explosion, the lynxes may have headed south in search of new sources of food.

Most of the lynxes shot or captured seemed to be in good health, with strong, hard, unworn teeth. Moreover, the roaming lynxes seemed relatively unafraid of human beings. All this suggested that the cats had spent most of their lives until then in the wilderness.

The visiting lynxes were particularly bold—hunting openly around barnyards and even suburban back yards. Unfortunately for farmers and home owners, the wildcat will eat almost anything it can kill, including house pets and poultry.

At the same time, farmers in Australia were facing a similar crisis. For the second year in a row, hordes of hungry mice had invaded the grainfields of Queensland.

The common house mouse, although small in size, poses a giant problem for the Australians. Periodically, populations of these mice explode and they overrun fields and farms. In 1972, the mice became a plague. Millions of the gluttonous rodents ate their way over the land, chewing up much of the winter wheat crop. Then they turned to the summer crops, such as sunflowers and sorghum. Finally, they nibbled their way into stored crops at granaries and mills.

How to counteract these "invasions" on opposite sides of the globe? No one has come up with viable solutions, but one suggestion—made jokingly, of course—was that the cat and mouse problem could be solved simply by sending the Canadian lynxes to Australia!

THE FALLING FISHES

A very strange rainfall over Australia's Northern Territory in February 1974 had ichthyologists as well as meteorologists scratching their heads. That's right, *ichthyologists*—those scientists who study fish—joined the Aussie weathermen in trying to explain why hundreds of small fish fell from the skies over a desolate area of the so-called "outback," miles away from any water.

Bill Tapp, a rugged rancher who runs the sprawling Killarney cattle station (or ranch) near the remote settlement of Katherine, reported that several hundred fish, all about 2 to 3 inches in length, had rained down on his land.

Rancher Tapp claimed the fabulous fish falls occurred during a violent tropical storm associated with the annual autumn rains. (Remember, the seasons are reversed "Down Under!")

Scores of fish fell near Tapp's ranch house, creating the odd and unbelievable sight of tiny silver fish flopping about in the dust and dirt of a normally parched desertlike land.

Officials at the Australian weather bureau speculate that the fish deluge may have resulted from a weird combination of tornado and thunderstorm, not at all uncommon in this part of the country at this time of the year.

Such a frightening combination often creates waterspouts over the sea. These whirlwinds are powerful enough to suck up water, seaweed, bits of driftwood, and even whole schools of fish floating near the surface.

These strong winds may then blow this watery mixture of flotsam and jetsam inland to fall on unsuspecting farmers, aborigines, and kangaroos strolling through the otherwise dry and barren scrublands of "outback."

Weather watchers in Darwin, Australia, claim that cases of falling fish are fairly regular occurrences in the Northern Territory and Queensland. In fact, Rancher Bill Tapp didn't seem too concerned about the finny rainfall in his back yard. When the Center for Short-Lived Phenomena asked him for more information about this unusual downpour of fish, he replied simply: "They look like perch."

Perhaps in that upside-down land, where the seasons are backward, and the everyday animals are kangaroos and koala bears, dingos and duckbilled platypuses, the unusual becomes commonplace and the odd-ball is oftentimes old hat.

THE TALE OF THE WHITE-TAILED RATS

The reports sounded terrifying . . . Thousands of rampaging rats had invaded the island of Formentera in the Mediterranean. Or had they? The true tale of the white-tailed rat invasion apparently depended on who was telling it.

According to angry and excited farmers on this tiny island off the coast of Spain, hordes of hungry rats were eating their way through vegetable, grain, and fruit crops and threatening to destroy the island's entire food supply.

On the other hand, calmer and cooler scientific experts claimed there was no "invasion," the number of rodents was not unusual, there was little or no damage to food supplies, and, indeed, *the rats really were not even rats!*

First reports of the so-called rat invasion reached the Smithsonian Center in late December 1971, when Formentera farmers requested government help in combatting an apparent plague of white-tailed rodents.

The Spanish government took no immediate action, but it did ask zoologists from the University of Barcelona to investigate the situation on Formentera. The island is part of the Balearic chain, a string of green jewels off Spain's Costa del Sol which attract thousands of tourists yearly. A rat plague would be disastrous, especially if it spread to the more popular island resorts on Mallorca.

Fortunately, the scientists found little cause for alarm. First, the rodents in question turned out to be a special breed of garden dormouse with long, white tails and an equally long Latin name *(Eliomys quercinus ophisuae)*, that lives only on Formentera.

Because the squirrel-like dormouse is unique to Formentera, it obviously couldn't be "invading" from somewhere else.

Moreover, zoologists claim even the hungriest dormice seldom dine on farm crops. Their normal diet consists of small animals, such as lizards and other mice, occasionally spiced with spiders, beetles, and assorted insects.

A bumper crop of little white-tailed dormice the previous year may have produced a minor population explosion when the rodents awoke from hibernation, convincing farmers an "invasion" was underway. More likely, the farmers of Formentera were looking for some government aid and the reports of "severe crop damage" could have been exaggerations designed to gain sympathy for their cause.

No steps were taken to exterminate the rodents. Government officials—at the suggestion of zoologists—wisely decided that any attempts to eliminate the dormice would only upset the island's delicate ecological balance.

FIRE AND ICE

The Aysen Province of southern Chile, one of the most forbidding and rugged areas of the world, almost appears as part of another, more evil planet. A mixture of towering peaks, dark lifeless valleys, and jagged coastline, this part of Chile resembles the shattered backbone of some crippled giant. Here, as the South American continent reaches out to the Antarctic, the great Andes Mountains drop straight into the sea and the landscape becomes a jumbled mixture of water, rock, and ice.

Few men either care—or dare—to tempt nature by living here. The province is as deserted as it is barren. There are no large cities and only a few villages. Rough dirt trails lead up into the few mountain valleys where hardy breeds of both cattle and men live in a constant battle against the elements.

In 1971, the people of the Huemules Valley in Aysen Province were struggling through the last days of the Southern Hemisphere's winter. Their hopes—and, indeed, their very survival—were pinned on the early arrival of spring. But it was not spring's warmth that would arrive unexpectedly in the Huemules Valley. Instead, it was the burning, searing, killing heat of a volcano.

On August 12, the Hudson Volcano high above the headwaters of the Huemules River erupted violently without warning, sending a smoke cloud more than 15,000 feet into the air, spewing hot ashes over some 60 square miles of land, and sending rivers of lava pouring down the valley.

For more than a week, eruption after eruption shattered the quiet of the mountains, and a steady stream of red-hot lava flowed over fields and pastures, cutting off roads, damming rivers, and levelling the flimsy stone and wood huts of the simple cattle herders.

More than 10,000 head of cattle and sheep were driven from the valley by the lava, but many others died in the steaming flows. Still other livestock, trapped in canyons and arroyos, slowly starved to death as a thick layer of ashes covered their meagre grazing lands.

To complicate the problems, the eruption's heat melted ice and snow on the volcano's slopes and on nearby glaciers, so that avalanches of mud, water, and ice rolled down the steep mountainsides in the wake of the lava flow.

Because the valley is so sparsely populated, the human death toll was relatively small. Still, the Smithsonian learned that only a handful of the fifty scattered families in the valley survived.

Some day those few men and women who managed to live through that terrifying week of "fire and ice," may come down from their mountains and tell what it was like to have seen "hell on earth."

LIFE IN SPACE?

The farmhands cursed the early morning heat of the Australian spring as they stacked hay in a barn near Murchison, Victoria. Suddenly, a low rumbling noise like thunder shook the barn, although no storm clouds appeared in the sky. Seconds later, a small dark stone crashed through the barn's roof and narrowly missed striking one of the farmers.

The men picked up the cool smooth rock. It was unusually heavy for its size and covered with a thin, black crust as if scorched in a fire. One edge of the rock had broken off, revealing a greyish cementlike interior flecked with bright metal dots. Most strange, the stone gave off the peculiar aroma of denatured alcohol.

Puzzled and perplexed, the men tried to explain how this unusual rock had come hurtling into their hayrack. Little did they know that they held a meteorite—a piece of cosmic debris probably left over from the breakup of some ancient planet. Nor could they imagine that this little stone from the sky would produce one of the most exciting scientific discoveries in history.

More than thirty fragments of what is now called the "Murchison Meteorite Fall" eventually were recovered near this Australian town. Most fell on a dirt road, but several others—like the barn stone—literally fell in the laps of some men standing around the concrete parking lot of an adjacent dairy.

The meteorites fell after a spectacular fireball streaked over southeastern Australia in broad daylight on September 28, 1969. Thousands of people watched this giant meteor with its long trail of smoke and dust enter the atmosphere and explode in midair.

Learning of the fireball and the recovered meteorites, the Smithsonian contacted Australian officials and arranged for samples to be distributed to research laboratories in the United States and elsewhere.

Scientists quickly identified the meteorites as carbonaceous chondrites, a rare type of meteorite rich in carbon materials and long thought to contain some clues to the origin of life in the solar system. Unfortunately, no real evidence had ever been found to prove this theory.

But this time, the scientists found their proof.

Little more than a year after the space stones crashed on earth, scientists at the National Aeronautics and Space Administration announced they had detected the presence of amino acids in the meteorites. Amino acids are complex organic compounds that form the basic building blocks of life, and this was the first time they had ever been found in a meteorite.

That little black rock found in the Australian hayrack may prove to be one of the most important pieces in the intricate puzzle of how life began.